# IDENTITY AND COMMUNITY
# IN THE GAY WORLD

# IDENTITY AND COMMUNITY IN THE GAY WORLD

CAROL A. B. WARREN

A WILEY-INTERSCIENCE PUBLICATION

JOHN WILEY & SONS New York • London • Sidney • Toronto

**Library of Congress Cataloging in Publication Data:**

Warren, Carol A    B      1944–
   Identity and community in the gay world.

   "A Wiley-Interscience publication."
   Bibliography: p.
   1.   Homosexuality—United States.   2.  Community.
I.  Title.

HQ76.3.U5W37      301.41'57      73-18121
ISBN 0-471-92112-2

Printed in the United States of America

10  9  8  7  6  5  4  3  2  1

TO THE GAY COMMUNITY

# PREFACE

*Identity and Community in the Gay World* is an ethnographic and theoretical study of each element in the title: identity, community, world, and gayness. The specific people, places, and times of the book must, in a society that stigmatizes homosexuals, remain anonymous; however, the book includes observational data from several hundred men and a few dozen women in a Western city I have called Sun City, during 1968–1973.

The widest focus of the book is world, and the narrowest is identity. All of us live in worlds, and some of us have identities. A world is a unit of experience, such as work, the gay world, or the family, which exists before we enter it and continues if we leave it; identity is a clear answer to the questions Who am I? and Where do I belong? Although worlds are wide open to observation, identities often remain elusive.

Some of the most fortunate of us, in the anonymity of mass society, have identities, and for many of us the identity we choose is clearly linked with community. As I have shown in this book, community is a matter of time, space, interaction and human relationships, and special knowledge, but it is also a matter of the sharing of a bond of fellowship that transcends concrete situations.

The gay community, like some others, is stigmatized by the larger society. Because of this, the experience of being and becoming gay, and the gay world and community itself, take on a fateful cast; the bond of fellowship is strengthened both by secret bearing of the stigma and by public declaration of it. Identity is forged within community, community within world, and world, ultimately, within the limits of contemporary society.

The methods of this book are participant observation of the gay community, supplemented by interviews of many of those who identify as gay but who choose to bear their stigma in secrecy from the straight world. Thus the scope of the study is limited not only in time and place but also with reference to the members' adaptation to stigma. My findings apply to other secret gay communities such as those studied by Evelyn Hooker (1963; 1965), Simon and Gagnon (1967; 1968), and others, but they cannot be generalized to the new generation of stigma confronting gay liberation activists (see Humphreys, 1971; 1972).

I am deeply indebted, first, to the people without whom this study could not have been written: the gay community and my close friends among them. I am also indebted to my advisors for their help and criticism: Professors Jack Douglas, Joseph Gusfield and Stanford Lyman of the University of California at San Diego, and Professors Joann DeLora and Dale Johnson of California State University at San Diego. Grateful thanks also to my Wiley-Interscience editor, Eric Valentine, for his cooperation and patience, and to Professor Arthur

Vidich for his helpful suggestions. My particular debt is to Professor Douglas, who provided an intellectual challenge in the earliest days of this book, and in a very real sense made it all possible.

Carol A. B. Warren
University of Southern California

*Los Angeles, California*
*August 1973*

# CONTENTS

# IDENTITY AND COMMUNITY
## IN THE GAY WORLD

# 1. THE GAY WORLD

STIGMA AND SECRECY. The gay world, like other worlds, is a unit of experience. Once a set of experiences is defined as a whole, the individual comes to act toward that whole and within it in certain expected ways. The world of work is entered at 9 AM and left at 5 PM, entered at age 20 and left at age 65, and requires certain task performances, skills, relationships, and presentations of self. The gay world has general features too. It is perceived by the gay individual as a whole, with a past and future existence independent of his experiencing of it; he acts toward that world, and within it, as a member, in certain expected ways.

The gay world itself is not a community of people, a set of relationships, or a spatial entity, although it is usually experienced with others, in special relationships and in

3

particular places. This book is about the gay world as a general experience and about a particular gay community sharing that experience, during 1968–1972, in a western beach city I call Sun City.

In general, the gay world has two distinctions. It is almost universally stigmatized, and no one is socialized within or toward it as a child. As used brilliantly by Erving Goffman, the term stigma refers to an attribute possessed by an individual that actually or potentially causes an audience to treat that person badly, label him as a deviant, or even arrest and convict him of a criminal offense. Some stigmata, such as dwarfism or paraplegia, cannot be hidden. These people who are stigmatized are described by Goffman as *discredited* persons. Other stigmata, such as homosexuality and a criminal record, render the holder only potentially stigmatized, or, in Goffman's terminology, *discreditable* (Goffman,1963).

I believe that nobody who now identifies himself or herself as a part of that world was deliberately socialized to become a homosexual. This makes the gay experience of stigma particularly significant and sociologically interesting. No one can argue, as many have done with reference to delinquents or criminals, that gay people have been brought up with roles, values, and behaviors radically different from those of straight people. Belonging to the gay world always entails a choice, often a difficult one.

After that choice comes another one: to be secret and discreditable, or to be open and discredited. The people in *this* study have made the choice of discreditability. Except when they are in the gay world they keep secret and conceal their homosexual preferences and their gay lifestyle. At work, with their mothers and fathers, at church, walking along the beach, these people attempt to be, and from my observations usually are, indistinguishable from straight people.

Secrecy, for the gay community, entails both sacrifices and delights. Gay persons must give up a whole range of options open to straight people but not to gay people who choose secrecy, such as holding hands with one's lover on the beach, honest communication with one's parents, truthful statements to work colleagues about how the weekend was spent. Other options are closed to all gay people by political fiat: marriage to a member of the same sex, adoption of children, family memberships in travel clubs, and tax breaks.

The delights of secrecy reside in the amplification of the gay experience, a *further* amplification of an experience which already assumes great significance because of the stigmatization of the rest of society. The overt adaptation to stigmatization makes the gay world more important to its members than other worlds; the secret response, I feel, adds excitement to stigma and makes the gay world doubly important.

Alone among sociologists, Georg Simmel recognized the fascination and power of secrecy, and its role in the creation of close communities and stable identities. He argues, first, that secrecy seduces by the tension between the necessity to conceal the stigma and the desire to confess it, which gives the unique trust generated between members an edge of danger. Although secrecy is essentially an individual phenomenon, the sharing of a secret makes interaction between the sharers the most important facet of their lives.

The secret world, especially the world whose secret is a feared stigma, fosters a clear-cut identity as well as a close-knit community. By the necessary exclusion of most outsiders from the group, secrecy clearly defines that secret as the centrally important facet of the self. Furthermore, society has already taught the stigmatized that a stigma is, like leprosy, a feature of the entire self, not confined to certain times, places, or acts. A person who engages in deviant behavior and is stigmatized is redefined as essentially different from normals, "having really always been that way all along," and undoubtedly going to be that way always.

A final seduction of the secret world is that it fosters the sense of an elite, chosen-people status, which Simmel calls the "aristocratizing principle." Often the stigmatization of the surrounding, hostile society is used in a kind of martyrdom of the elect, breeding a heightened sense of both superiority and unjust persecution. The Jews of the diaspora, the black community, and the gay community exemplify the aristocratizing effect of stigma and secrecy.

A related effect of aristocratizing is equality among members, coupled with high valuation on association with other members. These three features of secrecy reduce conflict between members and negate conflict between the demands of the gay and other worlds, since the gay world so clearly remains the most important one. Conformity to the norms of that world and excellence at its interaction rituals become extremely important to the member, whose membership may be said to be his most precious possession (Simmel, 1950, pp. 358–359).

LABELING THEORY AND POWER.   Within contemporary sociology, although the concept of stigma is used as a sensitizing idea by many, the labeling theory of deviance (which deals with aspects of the same phenomenon of audience response to deviant behavior) is the major theoretical perspective in the field, analogous in glamor and seductiveness (if the analogy may be pardoned) to the secret gay community.

However, the labeling theory of deviance in the form in which it has traditionally been stated is clearly not applicable to the gay world as interpreted here by the twin concepts of stigma and secrecy. Labeling theory, in its classic formulations by Becker and Lemert, involves two main propositions. Deviance is not a quality of an act or actor but is a product of the application of rules backed by institutionalized social power. The application of that power "escalates" the labeled person to more deviant behavior, and to a stigmatized identity and way of life (Becker, 1963; Lemert, 1967). The differentiation between this theory and the perspective of stigma and secrecy is threefold. First, power resides in secrecy as well as in public stigmatization, and in interaction as well as institutions. Second, the individual may proceed to further deviant behavior and a stigmatized identity and way of life without the intervention of concrete social labeling. Third, the individual is a free social actor with choices and possibilities, and is not determined in his future actions and identities by the social labels of any person or group, no matter how powerful. To illustrate:

> Irwin, who was from a very conservative and religious background, developed a sexual relationship with the next-door neighbor man, which was carried on for several months before his wife found the couple *in flagrante delicto*. The ensuing divorce was painful to Irwin, since his wife prevented him from gaining visitation rights to their three children by labeling him "homosexual" in court. For the next four years, Irwin continued the sexual relationship with the other man, but searched for a new wife, since he still defined himself as a heterosexual who "happened" to have had this "unique" sexual relationship and happened to get caught. It was not until he met a man who was a member of the gay community that he learned to define himself as gay. (Condensed from a case study.)

Although this case cannot be said to be representative, and is in fact unique in my experience (none of the other members had been publicly labeled homosexual), it illustrates a couple of these points quite effectively. First, the individual social actor *responds* to institutionalized power and social labels in ways that vary with his choices and circumstances. We have already observed the making of a choice between overt and secret gayness; in this instance, Irwin, despite public labeling, was not brought to *that* choice because he *chose not to accept the label.*

Later Irwin came to label himself as gay and find a place within the gay world, which indeed is the most usual route to a gay identity. The power of the gay world, in this case the secret gay community, transcended that of the straight world, despite their quite different institutionalized and political strengths.

A much more typical experience is the following:

> Nelson was brought up in a highly conservative Midwestern family, and went to college on the West coast at the age of seventeen. He developed a strong sexual attraction for his roommate, which disturbed him greatly, and he decided he must be sinful, or sick, or both. He went for help to the counselors at the college, to the minister of the church he attended, and to the library, and got much conflicting advice plus the label "homosexual." Later in his college experience, he became attracted to a man who was a member of the gay community and introduced him to homosexuality and the gay world. Nelson fought this involvement, but eventually became a confirmed, committed secret gay, with a lover, a house, and two dogs. (Condensed from a case study.)

Nelson, unlike Irwin, labeled himself (tentatively) a homosexual before labeling by any external social audience, and was never publicly labeled by the criminal justice system; he reached his gayness by a process which I refer to elsewhere as symbolic labeling (Warren and Johnson, 1972). However, he initially accepted society's definition of homosexuality as a stigma, with all the negative connotations of sickness, sinfulness, and evil. It remained for the gay community both to consolidate his identity and lifestyle and to transform that stigma into something positive and valuable.

For these and other reasons, labeling theory is inadequate for a true understanding of the gay community, although it purports to explain the development of stigmatized identities and lifestyles in general. Furthermore, labeling theory relies for its impact on the premise that audiences will react to deviant behavior, and that the reaction will be negative. Empirical work has clearly shown that people prefer to ignore deviant behavior and not stigmatize the perpetrators, though they may indeed harbor nasty thoughts (Kitsuse, 1964; Emerson, 1970). Socialization into the straight world and the torment of negative self-feelings is often more powerful in stigmatization than the reaction of *any* audience.

THEMES AND BIASES. Several identifiable themes have emerged from this discussion of stigma, secrecy, and labeling theory; these themes are continued throughout the chapters that follow. One theme is identity as a person experiences it and others impute it. A linked theme is community and how it facilitates the development of a gay identity. A final theme, in a sense framing all the others, is society, which needs a more careful definition.

In traditional sociology, "society" is used to refer to a social system that transcends both individuals and communities, with a life and will of its own, by which all selves and all communities are utlimately determined. *In this context*, the term society is used to refer to *the concept people have that this is so.* As long as people think that they are the product of their environment, or their heredity, or of the power elite, this concept will affect their lives. As W.I. Thomas said (in a phrase that now sounds boring but remains true):

"Things that are defined as real are real in their consequences." The question of whether society is "real" or not is in
a sense irrelevant; what is important is that gay people,
among others, regard society as a force to be reckoned with.
The theme of community, too, needs further clarification.
As used here, it refers both to the general characteristics of
any community (facilitating the interaction of members, providing an identity, and so on) and to the specific people
around whom the study was built. When I use the term "the
community," or "the gay community," then, I am referring to
what the particular community taught me about the general
characteristics of community, *and* what set it off from other
types of gay community. This serves to remind the reader
that the general principles are always qualified by the fact
that they were worked out in specific times, places, and with
specific people in unique relationships with myself as a
person.

The biases, or as I prefer to call them philosophy of life implied by these statements, are discussed with reference to
methodology in the Appendix. But they also affect the
perspective from which I viewed the gay world, and the
frame I placed around it in presentation to the reader.

The frame is phenomenological; the perspective,
existential. The findings here are framed, as far as possible,
with reference to *the meanings of the gay world as the
members experienced it*, although, of course, these meanings
are transformed into a sociological presentation by the addition of theorizing. The existential perspective is, quite
simply, a nondeterministic view of people and their identities.
In this sense, it *is* relevant whether or not society is perceived
as a real entity, with deterministic power; it is important to
state that my bias is opposed to the traditional perspective.

Social theory too often implies that individuals are pawns
of fate in the shape of the social system, just as psychological
theory sees people as pawns of fate in shapes such as the

unconscious or driving motivations, or religion views them as possessed by demons, or vessels of the holy spirit. Existentialism sees all these things as important, up to and including the demons, but asserts the free will, choice, and responsibility of the actor in response to society, religion, or drives. Identity is created, not assigned.

This has implications for sociology as an enterprise, in that sociologists are subject to the same interpretation. Whereas traditional sociologists have sought to present an "objective" social world "out there" and "as it really is" by the progressive elimination of subjectivity and bias, other sociologists including myself take the existential position that the act of perception is an intrinsic part of the findings, and the two are not separable into subject and object. The sociologist, while also a phenomenologist attempting to view the world from the members' perspective, remains an actor in the social world he is describing, with all the personal emotions, effects, relationships, problems, and pitfalls of the other actors. Experience is not confined to members but extends to us, the analysts of it.

# I.  COMMUNITY

A community is an idea, as well as a group of people. The essence of the idea is psychic; those who form a community, whether it is one of tradition, ethnicity, or sexuality, have a sense of oneness, of brotherhood or sisterhood. But people, in relationships, live out the idea of community.

The people who formed the gay community I studied lived in a particular place, at a particular time, but the gay community is not bounded by places and times because gay people do not have to live together to feel a sense of community; secrecy and stigma give them that. The boundaries of place and time, then, serve only to locate the particular people; descriptions of their relationships, interaction, and knowledge are also specific to the group but do not depend on it for their form.

I kept no count of the people I knew scarcely, quite well, and closely; there might be several hundred mere acquaintances, eighty known at the level of sociability, and several dozen who have been (and some who still are) close friends within the limits of geography and changing experiences. The research covered a period of several years in which I spent much of my leisure time within the gay world, and the places were homes and public spaces in Sun City, as many as I could get into without risk to self or safety (which means no rest rooms, no Turkish baths).

The knowledge I slowly accumulated about the community as the members experienced it was of a peculiar sort, as I realized when I showed some of them this book in various stages of preparation. Reactions were diverse, including condemnation, agreement, lack of understanding, and amazement. This is inevitable, since people do disagree with one another, even about worlds they commonly inhabit. My sociologist's knowledge, then, is like theirs—shared with others, but representing only a fragment of the meanings that are possible within that world.

Space, time, interaction, relationship, and knowledge are the elements of community—but they do not fully describe a community. Added to these dimensions are the unique self and the psychic experience for each individual of gay worlds and others: these are never forgotten in the pages that follow, but they are given clearest focus in Parts II and III.

# 2. SPACE AND TIME

Space and time are the concrete boundaries of a community, in a not quite metaphorical sense. A community that is secret and stigmatized must quite literally have walls: places and times set apart from other places and times in which the community can celebrate itself. Although gay places are always specific and can be found, gay time may be spent internally, invisible from the world around, as well as externally, within gay places.

Walls imply walling out as well as walling in; gay people learn to wall themselves out of straight places. Whereas straight people may find companionship, sex, and lifetime love in all kinds of settings, from church to the workplace, secret gay people may neither find others like themselves there, nor be gay in those settings. Gay people who cannot find gay settings remain isolated, outside the straight world and not within the gay one:

> KIM: Before I found the gay bar* I knew that I was a homosexual but there was nowhere for me to go and meet others. I would often just roam the streets, riding on buses and walking, looking for a face that might be sympathetic. I literally did not know what to do. (Conversation)

Gay time may be spent within gay spaces or inside the self, walled off from the surrounding straight setting. Externally, and beyond the general boundaries of our social calendar and 24-hour time clock, social time in our society is divided into experience phases: worlds of work and leisure and sleep. It is characteristic of the twentieth century that leisure time expands as work lessens.

The gay community exists within leisure time, since the contexts of stigma and secrecy prevent its extension into work time. The gay world, then, is a world of leisure time, structured by the concept of leisure and play, and giving a value to leisure beyond simple relaxation. By confinement to leisure time, and through the centrality of the gay experience, sociability and play become the most significant of life's tasks.

The stigmatization of the gay world ensures that all gay space and time will tend toward secrecy. Gay inner time and gay interaction are protected from the invasion of outsiders by other kinds of walls: the refusal of entry to strangers, the concealment of gay bar entrances, and the palpable change that happens in a gay crowd on the entry of straights. In this way, gay time spent within gay spaces gains a highly exclusive, trusting, and valuable character by its very secrecy.

---

* A bar whose patronage is predominantly homosexual, and which is gay in atmosphere and reputation.

SPACE. There are both public and private gay places where gay identity may be exposed in every town and probably every village of the nation. Private spaces are primarily people's homes and a few private clubs, and there are public bars, streets, parks, beaches, baths, gyms, movie houses, motels, tearooms,* and bars. Just about every community has at least one gay or mixed† bar, since bars are the most important public community places.

Gay community members know about the types of places likely to be gay, and they find specific gay places by word-of-mouth recommendations and, especially when they are traveling, from published gay guides. There are several of these, published yearly, covering various territories of the United States and other countries. International bar guides list gay bars, baths, and other institutions in countries where the police are lenient to the gay community (most of Western Europe), and also good cruising spots‡, from parks to hotel lobbies. In Roman Catholic and Eastern European countries, where specifically gay places are discouraged, entries list only cruising spots and places where gays congregate (always Hilton hotels and Dennys). In the nations of Asia and Africa, gays are told where to find such specialities as male brothels and male children.

Other guides cover the United States as a whole, geographical regions of the west or north, or individual states. Since particular bars shift in clientele from gay to straight, go broke, disappear, or change in atmosphere, the bar guides are always out of date and often prove less useful than recommendations:

> We searched for bars listed in last year's San Francisco
> gay guide entry. The first one was just not there; the

* Men's rest rooms noted for homosexual activity (see, for example, Humphreys, 1970).
† Bars with some gay patronage.
‡ Places known for homosexual pickups.

area's buildings were being torn down. The second had become a straight bar with go-go entertainment. The third was still there and still gay, but the guide designated it as "elegant," and it certainly wasn't. (From field notes)

The gay guides not only list the addresses of bars and other places but also give some indication of the type of atmosphere and clientele. In one guide, bars are classified by the following symbols:

D    Dancing
R    Restaurant
G    Gay girls' bar
M    Mixed straight and gay
H    Hippie or collegiate; young crowd
E    Elegant; coat and tie may be required
C    Coffee bar only
L    Liquor bar
B    Beer, or beer and wine only served
SM   Sadomasochist or leather crowd*
W    Western-type attire†
*    Popular

In many cities, including Sun City, gay bars and homes are clustered in the same areas. Some areas have so many gay people that the gay community gives them special names, like the "Swish Alps" for one particular part of Los Angeles; some streets and apartment buildings become all-gay or have a majority of gay dwellers. In Sun City there are several major areas of gay residence: downtown among the city's gay and

---

* A gay person who is "leather" is either sado-masochistic by sexual preference or wears the kind of clothes popular among S & Ms: leather jackets and pants, or motorcycle gear.

† In some bars, the men costume themselves in Western attire: boots and spurs, breeches, cowboy hats. This does not indicate a sexual act perference.

straight night life, an upper-middle-class suburb, and an adjacent beach area, all of which have gay bars.

*Gay Bars.* Gay bars are most significant for community activity for many reasons. First, they are sexually defining spaces. Anyone inside them is presumed to be gay, and, if male, a legitimate object for a sexual advance.* There are few other places in our society where this is true for homosexuals; settings of work, family, or church seem dangerous to secret gays in search of sex:

> JASON: I've always had a hang-up against approaching anyone unless they were in a gay context so that the context would do the definition for me.... I've never revealed my preferences to anyone who wasn't gay—well, with a couple of exceptions—with a very few exceptions—and I really get uptight about the prospect of doing that, and trying to approach people in a straight situation, where, you don't know about them, might lay you open to that kind of exposure which—which I just wouldn't like to do. (Tape-recorded interview)

Bars are used not only to make sexual contacts, but to expand the circle of sociability:

> CAROL: What is your motivation to go to gay bars?
> JASON: The motivation is—to—to—meet people, it's not to drink, or its not to, you know, just go out for the sake of going out. It always has a purpose behind it—the purpose is not necessarily looking for sex either, but it's, you know, to meet new people, and, you know, have these acquaintances lead where they may, whether you might have sex that night, or get to meet

---

* Contrary to public stereotypes, such advances usually take the form of glances, not instant attack.

someone who's a friend, or whatever. (Tape-recorded interview)

OLIVER: When I want to pick up a trick I go to the Den, but the Flyover is best to meet new people. (conversation)

Bars are also places to greet members of the clique networks to which gay people belong and continue sociable relations (see Chapters 4 and 5). This function is in tension with sexual and sociable searching, since talking to acquaintances can prevent meeting new people, and talking to new people in front of cronies can be embarrassing:

JASON: Gay circles can be sort of gossipy and closed, and there tends to be a great deal of talk and gossip outside the bars about—"well, I saw so-and-so in the bar, and he picked up on a certain type of guy, and that's his hang up," or something like that, or—you're talked about all the time, people try to construct patterns out of your behavior and so forth which, you know, I dislike—there's a great deal of emphasis placed on making it, you know, and finding an attractive guy to go with, and so forth, and, er, as I say it's a thing which you're being tested so to speak in front of everybody else, and you know I just don't like to feel that way. (Tape-recorded interview)

Because of their multiple functions, gay bars become specialized. As Oliver said, the Den is a cruising bar and the Flyover is a bar popular with people from out of town; other bars are popular with blacks, or sailors, and still others are home territory bars for particular cliques.*

Whatever their particular clientele and reputation, however, gay bars are places in which gay identities are created and

* A home territory bar is patronized by the same people over long periods of time (see Cavan, 1965).

sustained for the self and others, by the self and others.
People in gay bars who know where they are (and most of
them do) assume that the others present are gay, which
means that many people in professional or business occupations are fearful about going to gay bars because of the
possible violation of their secrecy. Contextual labeling of this
kind is particularly likely in mixed bars that have a reputation
in straight circles (such as bars featuring drag shows†),
where a secret gay may run into straight business acquaintances out on the town.

Members of the secret gay community vary in the degree
to which they boycott gay bars in fear of exposure. Gary, for
example, says:

> Although I sometimes go to Christophers, I never go to
> Midlands or Kenos (drag show bars) because I might
> run into other faculty there, or parents, or students who
> graduated. I sometimes go to the Flyover, but it makes
> me uncomfortable. In that part of town, anybody might
> walk in. (Conversation)

But Peter, who is also a teacher, disagrees:

> PETER: I go everywhere. I say, if they are there, its for
> the same reason I am. (Conversation)

Although a few members refuse to go to any bar, most do so
from time to time, and some indeed have had the experience
of running into straight acquaintances:

> BRENTON: Oh sure I have run into people I know in
> gay bars—it's too small a town not to. Particularly
> when you teach high school. I've seen lots of kids in
> there, and usually I've already picked them out. (Con-
> versation)

† Shows with female impersonators.

Labeling is not just done by others in bars, it is done by the self. Many people "come out," in the sense of identifying themselves as gay people, in gay bars. Hooker calls this the "socialization function" of gay bars, and, as important as the bars are for coming out, they would be more so if the drinking age were lower (Hooker, 1967; Dank, 1971). In Dank's study, although 50 percent reported that they had come out through association with other gay people, only 19 percent of his sample had done so in bars. Most had come out before they were 21 years old, in other kinds of places (Dank, 1971, pp. 181–184).

As Hooker adds, "the bar system is relatively stable" (1967, p. 173). Gay bars are found in most sizable cities, and they open and close generally in areas where previous gay bars have attracted gay homes. Rarely are gay bars opened in areas of the city not having gay colonies, and rarely do·gay people take over an existing straight bar as their own (Achilles, 1967 pp. 228–244). Hooker points out that although the system is stable, the actual bars are not, but that was in Los Angeles. In Sun City, both the system and the bars are stable: of the approximately thirteen gay bars operating in 1968, nine were still in operation in 1973. Some had closed, and there were some new ones too.

There are mixed bars as well as gay bars in most cities, although not as many, because for secret gays the mixing of worlds can be uncomfortable. Some mixed bars are predominantly gay but have some straight clientele, such as the Sun City drag bars Midlands and Kenos. Others are predominantly straight but are patronized by a few gay people on a regular basis. Sometimes bars change in character from straight to gay, gay to straight, or mixed to straight or gay exclusively, but this is difficult because of the period of transition (see Lyman and Scott, 1970 pp. 92–93):

> Barbara's had been not just a go-go bar but a famous one until it was bought by a gay business and turned

into a gay bar a few months ago. As the bartender commented: "the sailors are always walking in here looking
for the girls, and boy do they get freaked out." (From
field notes)

The maintenance of a mixed bar is, if anything, even more
difficult than the transition from straight to gay and back. In
my observation, it can really only be accomplished with a
drag bar, for reasons suggested by Sherri Cavan (1965, pp.
155–160). In a bar with a show, the focus of eye attention is
the stage, and interaction is suspended. In such a situation,
two potentially colliding worlds can stay out of collision, and
more or less ignore one another.

Kenos and Midlands started as gay bars and advertised for
straight clients to make more money. In only one instance I
encountered did the management open a bar specifically to
attract both gays and straights, and in this instance it wasn't
even a drag bar:

> The ID checker at the door quickly scrutinized the in-
> coming crowd to ascertain the sexual characteristics of
> each entering person or couple. Straight people were
> sent to the large main restaurant, gay men to a
> somewhat smaller room, and gay women to a still
> smaller back room. I asked the checker how he knew;
> he said "I just know." People stayed where they were
> put; the few who did wander around were cooled out
> by those who belonged. The manager walked around at-
> tempting to sell private club membership to the gay
> people; for $15 a month they would get a key to the
> proposed gay club upstairs. To reach this club they
> would have to walk through the main dining room,
> which was to be prodominantly straight. (Field notes)

This was not a popular idea with the gay community, and
within a few months only the straight crowd patronized the
bar-restaurant. The gays did not like the idea of the

membership fee, or walking through the main dining room (which is hardly conducive to the keeping of a secret), or the stigmatization implied in the segregation of the gay group.

As this indicates, bar owners and managers have various problems in running a successful bar. The gay crowd, as many of the members point out, is basically fickle, and there are fashions in bar going. A bar which is full one week is empty the next, then full again some months later (if it hasn't closed) without a reason. This happens to both home territory and cruising bars; cruising bars because new faces quickly become old, and home territory bars because the communications network is so rapid that a whole group can shift from bar to bar with little trouble.

There is of course a variation in bar life, from a few that open and close with hardly a trace to bars that attract the same people for months and even years, and everything in between. In Sun City, Christophers (located in the upper-middle-class suburb of El Sol) is the most stable, with a changeless clientele of middle-class, middle-aged people who hardly vary with the decades. At the opposite extreme is the Flashlight, which has changed many times during the past four years from a gay men's to a gay women's bar and back, from a popular to an unpopular place and back.

One of the reasons for such fickleness, as Cavan points out, is that bars are used for various purposes, from sexual contacts to entertainment, so habit is not always the major factor. As already indicated, some bars are known for cruising, others for drag shows; still others are funky beer bars where lower-class tricks* can be picked up:

> OLIVER: I go to the Flyover, which is—over a few blocks—when I want to have a quick beer after work and see my friends, then on weekends when I don't have to get up I'll mostly go to the Den downtown—all

---

* Pickup for casual sex purposes.

those cute young things to pick from, and me such an
old man.
CAROL: The Den? That's a new one.
. . . do you ever go to Kenos?
OLIVER: No never. I don't care for the drag shows.
When you're footloose and single you have other things
on your mind. (Conversation)

CAROL: What did you do last night?
OLIVER: I went to the Flyover and ran into George—
you know, this guy I had a thing with years ago, and I'd
really like to get something going again—and then we
went to the Casket—
CAROL (interrupts, surprised, since the Casket is a gay
women's bar): What on earth were you doing there?
OLIVER: Frankly, I took him there because I didn't want
any competition. No danger of him running into a cute
trick at the Casket. (Conversation)

Bar owners and managers are aware of the problems they
face in running a predictable and profitable business; successful bars can make a fortune, although unsuccessful ones
have lost everything for their owners. They try all kinds of inducements to increase their patronage. One type of in-
ducement is financial, like happy hours with drinks for 40
cents, or Tuesday meals for $1.25, or parties with food "on
the house." Other inducements are atmospheric, like a live
band, a dance floor with a light show, or a pool table.

Very important, too, is the bar's personnel; its managers,
bartenders, and cocktail waiters and waitresses (and food
waiters and waitresses if it is also a restaurant). As Achilles
points out, "A particular owner may have operated several
bars, and a particular bartender may have been employed by
a dozen" (1967, p. 239); this is not necessarily because of
bar closures, but because bars raid one another for personnel.
The importance of personnel popularity, expecially the bar-

tender, is great, since he may take his following with him to the new bar; they say "Let's go see Bill," rather than "Let's go to the Den":

> I was surprised to see Charles tending night bar at Kenos, since he had for years been the day bartender at Christophers, and everyone was used to him. Kenos had also raided Midlands for some of their top drag performers, and their cocktail waitress, Katharine, who had also been at Christophers some years back. A few months later Charles was back at Christophers, saying that he couldn't stand the pace or the straight people. (From field notes)

Owners are as often straight as gay; for example, the owners of Christophers are a straight couple, and the owners of Midlands are a gay couple. Bartenders and cocktail and food waiters are almost always attractive young gay men, whereas the cocktail and food waitresses are almost always straight, and sometimes middle aged and motherly (like Katharine) rather than young and pretty. Whether bar personnel are gay or straight, the important thing is that they relate well to the gay community and do not stigmatize them (see also Cavan, 1965, pp. 226–227):

> "Ernie's"* . . . a good place not to go. Why should we support an establishment that has for so many years taken money and support of the gay clientele and yet never put a thing back into it, other than rotten service and sarcasm. Support your own!!! (*Exodus*, 1970, p. 13)

Not only must bar personnel be supportive, it helps if they are well known in the local gay community. Most bars that opened between 1968 and 1973 were opened by es-

* A downtown mixed bar.

tablished bar owners and succeeded fairly well, at least for a time; the two or three bars that were opened by out-of-towners did not do well at all:

> Flower Field opened near where I lived, and I went in a few times. It was a routine beer bar, with 24-cent draft, pool, and a small dance floor. There was never more than one person in there at any time, and several times there was just the bartender, watching his color television. He was from Los Angeles, and had opened the bar as a business venture. Within three months it had been sold and was a straight bar. (Field notes)

*Gay Homes.* Whereas the bars are the most important gay public places, the owned and rented homes of the gay community are the most important private spaces. Younger gay people do a lot of their socializing in gay bars; when they get older they entertain more in their own homes, which increasingly become the focus of their attention. The younger men claim that the older men drift into this pattern because they are no longer able to compete sexually in the marketplace of the gay bar, but the older men say it is because home entertainment is more intimate and rewarding:

> TIMOTHY (age 24): You know why these older guys say they don't go to the bars? They don't make out in the bars, that's why. The only place they can go is Christophers, there's no competition because they're all old. (conversation)

> JOHN (age 40):... but I prefer the gay crowd now, particularly my particular kind of people.
> CAROL: What do you mean by your particular kind of people?

JOHN: Uh—socializing on a home basis. Entertaining for cocktails in the home, going to people's houses for parties. I like to go to the bars, periodically, but—er— I'm not that interested in that particular socialization. I have more fun in a closer relationship with people rather than going and sitting in a bar all evening long and maybe talking to someone that you don't even know.

CAROL: Yes.

JOHN: Regardless of whether you want to take them home or not—but—at least at my age. It might be different if I was younger. (Tape-recorded interview)

Home socialization requires that the homes of gay people be of a particular style and (depending on the particular clique) of a certain scope. Older couples, in their late twenties, thirties, forties, and fifties, spend a large portion of their incomes in obtaining, decorating, and maintaining their homes for lifestyle and entertainment purposes, and, although many live in rented apartments and houses, the ideal is to own a home. Types of home include very expensive owned ($40,-000 and on up); expensive owned ($30,000–45,000); less expensive owned ($15,000–30,000) and rentals of various shapes and sizes:

Samuel and Dawson's house is in the newly developed part of Cahuenga, just north of Sun City, overlooking mountains and ocean. Its cost was probably somewhere in the $80,000 range, and I have no way of estimating the additional cost of the decoration. There is an Olympic size pool, surrounded by marble statuary, with a small guest house–cabana. Inside the house are three bedrooms and two bathrooms, all large. The dining room and kitchen have marble floors, while the enormous living room is furnished with at least three furniture groupings, all antiques or elaborate approximations. The green carpeting is soft and deep throughout.

Frederick and Darrell just moved into their new con-
dominium, which cost around $35,000. Frederick is
building a marble fountain in the backyard, and they are
busy putting down new shag carpeting (deep red). The
old carpeting looks new; they tell me "we like to lie
naked on the floor." They, like the other separate-
dwelling owners, have use of the gardenlike grounds, a
pool, sauna and tennis courts. Their house has two
bedrooms and two baths, and a good size living room.
The dining room is an angled corner of the living room
with a small chandelier to designate the spot for the
table, and the kitchen is visible from the dining room
(they plan to mirror the opening and hide it). They move
into a house like this, fix it up with marble fountains,
landscaping and new rugs, then sell it for hundreds of
dollars more than they paid, and buy a new one.

Justin lives in a small house in the fashionable part of El
Sol, which he rents but is trying to buy. It is small, but
has a fireplace in the living room and a lovely enclosed
patio. He has fixed it up in vivid yellows, black and
white with very little money; yellow vinyl cushions,
chairs with black and white animals, a gleaming dining
room table of black that is actually a painted picnic set,
topped by heavy silver chandeliers. There is a huge
round cocktail table with some very elegant crystal, and
fresh flowers. (From field notes)

Although these homes are quite different in scope, they
show similarities in style. The style is one of subdued
elegance and neatness, with exact placement of objects and
combinations of colors, textures, and surfaces; idiosyncratic
and personal touches; and great care, cleanliness, and
tidiness. The scope of this style, of course, varies from the
cleverly painted picnic tables and stools of the yellow, black,
and white living room to the most opulent elegance of
Samuel and Dawson. But the thread is there throughout.

Gay men, especially couples, will save and make sacrifices to own a home. One reason for this is that home ownership is the best way to preserve secrecy and privacy. Nosy neighbors cannot spy, and watchful landlords cannot evict. For the same reasons, those who do rent prefer houses to apartments.

Often, though, gay men make payments on homes which appear to be quite large in terms of their incomes. Moreover, the fixing up of these houses, with the kind of styles involved, also costs a lot of money, so many gay men learn to do their own gardening, plumbing, roofing, and even fountain building. The attractiveness, and especially the orderliness of gay men's homes never ceased to amaze me; the time spent in sociability is considerable, but the time spent setting the stage must also be great.

*Spaces and Masks.*   Whatever the gay space, however, the function is the same—a place where the expression of the true self can be allowed. This was most often expressed as "letting down my hair" or "being myself":

> JEROME: You get in a gay bar, I think, it gives you a chance to really let your hair down, and say, you know that you don't have to put on any kind of a facade, no one there is looking for you to be any one else but yourselves. (Conversation)

Restating the near-metaphor of the wall, gay places are where the walls can be allowed to fall, where the mask worn in straight interaction can be dropped, and where the secret gay can quite literally be himself:

> JOHN: At the present time I no longer work for the company that I used  to, and my association now with people is almost literally—with the gay set of people,

and as far as straight people are concerned, I see some
of my friends periodically, and I call them, but I—er—I
very seldom have any social obligations with them.
CAROL: Do you prefer this?
JOHN: Yes. It's much more comfortable for me now.
It's very difficult leading a double set of standards,
where you have to switch on and off so fast—and
particularly in your home. (Tape-recorded interview)

What Simmel describes quite concretely may be taken
symbolically with reference to the gay community: "an
outstanding expert suggested that the presence of masks
among a nature people should at once make one suspect the
existence of secret societies. It is . . . in the nature of the
secret order for the members to conceal themselves." (Simmel, 1950, p. 373). Although "nature people" wear quite real
physical masks to conceal their identities, secret gay people
wear quite real role-playing masks, which must be worn in all
straight spaces, and can only be dropped in gay ones.

*Territorial Invasion.*    Even the most secret spaces are not
completely protected from what Lyman and Scott call "territorial invasion . . . where those not entitled to entrance or use
nevertheless cross the boundaries and interrupt, halt, take
over or change the social meaning of the territory." Reactions
to this are varied: ignoring the newcomers, routing them, or
being overpowered by them (Lyman and Scott, 1970, pp.
99–102). In the gay world, territorial invasion may be by gay
people into straight places or by straight people into gay
places, and either can be unwitting or deliberate. Public
places are most likely to be invaded, but homes are not invio-
late:

A couple entered Kenos. He was young and crewcut;
she was clinging closely to his neck. They sat down, and

watched the drag show, which had just started, with an air of grim determination and an occasional nervous laugh. "Midwest tourists" murmured my neighbor.

Gerald invited two gay guys to come to dinner at his house and added "Alice and Tom will be there." To their quizzical looks he replied "It's OK. They're straight, but they're wise,* and they love the gay scene."

Oliver was recounting his recent dinner party with Bill and his wife Ann. Bill had been gay for years and a good friend of Oliver's, but a year ago, in his-mid thirties, he had married Ann. Ann was aware of Bill's past and of Oliver's homosexuality, but no one apparently wanted to talk about it. Oliver said "We couldn't talk about old times, or what the crowd was doing, or who was going with whom, or anything. We just sat there."

The Hi-Tide was crowded with people, and there were many couples on the dance floor—men with men, women with women, and men with women. Two heterosexual middle-aged couples came in, obviously left over from the time when the Hi-Tide was a straight restaurant. They headed for a table. Suddenly the lead man wheeled around and flailed his arms at his companions, shouting, "Oh my god, oh my god, we've got to get out of here—quick—hurry—oh my god!" They all rushed out.

Donald was relating how his mother had gone to the Warmup Room with another elderly lady who had known the Room when it was a popular Chinese restaurant. They found out that food was no longer served, so stayed only for a couple of pre-dinner cocktails. Donald related: "She said it seemed kind of strange—

* See Chapter 5.

she couldn't say exactly why. When I think I was there the previous evening. I almost died!"

JOHN: I was having a party one evening, and I was living alone at the time, it was when I first moved out to the beach, and I had about, oh, eight or ten people over at the house for dinner and as usual, when you get— uh—a few drinks under your belt, the talking gets very loud, and everyone's camping and carrying on,* and suddenly the doorbell rings, and its a very close friend of mine and his wife—-happened to be in the area and stopped by, and—you just—it's like a shot of adrenalin to you, you just don't know what to do, but you'd like to put tape over everyone's mouth for a few minutes, but you don't.

As these examples show, different circumstances lead to different reactions to territorial invasion. In Kenos, Midlands, and other drag bars, straight couples like the "Midwest tourists" are part of the setting, and gay people who want to go there get used to them. At the other end of the spectrum, Christophers has many tactics to prevent the entry of straight people, and to cool them out if they do enter:

> I was having dinner with a friend at Christophers, and noticed that the waiter was setting up the table next to us for three people. He put a "reserved" sign on it. I asked if that meant that three people I knew who dined frequently at Christophers were coming in, and he said: "No, no one's coming, but it keeps the straight people out." (Field notes)

> A man and wife that lived in the apartment building where I lived came into Christophers and sat down at a table. The bartender looked at them, but didn't ask them

* See Chapter 5.

what they wanted, and they did not go up to the bar. After twenty minutes of sitting and being ignored, they got up and left. (Field notes)

In other instances, the invaders may refuse to leave, and possibly even rout the habitués:

There were four women and a man in Casket when five men in leather jackets, boots, and caps came in. They clustered around the end of the bar close to the girls, and stood behind them shouting their drinks orders to the woman bartender. They talked and horsed around loudly for a few minutes as they were served. The women had been talking quietly when the five entered; now all were silent, and two moved to the other end of the bar. The man got up and left. (Field notes)

There is a possibly apocryphal story in the community that one night some years ago a group of men wielding baseball bats rushed into Christophers shouting "let's kill the queers," utterly routing the middle-aged patrons. (Anecdote)

Although gay people live in straight as well as gay worlds, they also sometimes invade straight space in the same ways. Gays may be secret tourists in the straight world, pretending to be straight but inwardly, or quietly together, laughing at all that the straights represent:

The group of two gay men and two gay women were planning a trip to a performance of the Soroptimists' club in El Sol. Noreen said: "What shall we wear?" They all agreed on very lavish and elegant clothing, and Jeremiah added: "We'll go and watch the straights do their thing. It should be good for a laugh. We'll look better than any of them." (Field notes)

Clearly, this kind of invasion retains the secrecy of the group; their activities are what Goffman calls "backstage." What distinguishes backstage gay invasions from simple interaction in the straight world is that the group would not pretend to be straight at the Soroptimists' performance, they would go as a group of gay people, cut off from the others by a wall of secrecy.

Lyman and Scott refer to this kind of backstage behavior as "time out," "a respite of the activities related to the time track . . . a period when roles and rules relating to the ongoing time track are relaxed or revoked" (Lyman and Scott, 1970, p. 204). Gay people in straight settings, when they take time out, quietly drop the mask of straightness and relax with other gays. This kind of thing happens quite a lot, and it helps cement community relationships even within the straight context. For example, at a Sun City community college there are several gay teachers who, although they do not all socialize on a regular basis in the gay world, meet as often as they can for lunch or coffee in the straight world, quietly turning a corner of the cafeteria into a gay backstage.

Not all gay time out in straight spaces is backstage or quiet, however. There are two kinds of frontstage gay invasion of straight space: overt and dramaturgical. Overt invasions, where gay people in straight places act in a way that will get them labeled, is sometimes deliberate (and of course secret gays don't do this) and sometimes accidental (usually a result of drunkenness):

> We all came together at Denny's for a very gay breakfast. The waitress can never be the same. We can't begin to tell you all the remarks that were made, but among the things that we noticed was an additional $20, added onto ——'s tab for the busboy. (*The Prodigal*, 1971, p. 5)

Eight people (including teachers and social welfare workers) from the secret gay community went into a Mexican restaurant, all very drunk from a cocktail party they had just left. Soon, they were loudly quarreling, shouting, some kissing. Kim sat on Darrell's knee, and their chair broke; Darrell threw it against the wall where it shattered. The group was thrown out and told never to come back. (Field notes)

Needless to say, they would not have done this in a purposeful way to freak out the restaurant—and, to my knowledge, none of them has ever been back.

Sometimes gay people may use the frontstage of a straight setting exactly as a stage, for the playing of a part, acting as a woman. This role gives the person a sense of freaking out the straights, but only through an inward satisfaction, since none of them knows that the "woman" is really a man. Thus, although overt and frontstage, passing as a woman has all the advantages of secrecy:

JEROME: It's more or less a game—and as I said again—possibly with a little bit of sarcasm, you know, you're saying to the people you have no idea—would that I stood up right now and took off this wig, and I said here I am a man, you know, you would have everything from giggles to laughs, you know, a complete variety of social reactions to this. But with them not knowing they're actually not looking for it, and if you're a decent looking drag it's even that much better—as I said, I have honestly no desire to be a woman so of course I feel like a man. It's more like I suppose an actor on a stage—it's a game—because when you're an actor and you're on a stage you're putting yourself into someone else's place and you're convincing the audience that you are what you are really not ... most kids have been in drag before.
CAROL: You have?

JEROME: It's sort of a kick, it's sort of a panic, you know, something different to do—to go socially out, which I have done, completely in drag, and go and mix with society in the nicest of restaurants and have no one have any idea that I'm a man, it's different, you know, it gives you sort of a feeling you can say, OK, now, because conventionally I look like a woman, here I am sitting here eating, and I'm being totally—er—accepted. (Tape-recorded interview)

Space is a most proprietory thing. Invasion of space in both contexts can increase the feeling of community among gay people. In the act of keeping others out of gay bars and homes, gay people reinforce the in-group–out-group division of the gay world, without challenging the stigma or the secrecy behind such actions. In the act of treating straight spaces either as unreal worlds or as stage settings for the invasion of outsiders, gay people continue to define themselves as outsiders, and as strangers to the straight world. As Robert Frost once said, walling in and walling out are aspects of one act.

TIME. Time is both internal and external. Take a man in the work world, performing a routine task and daydreaming about another world—his home. He may be thinking about his wife, his bills, his children; if a colleague interrupts and asks him what he is thinking, he says "Oh, about my wife and family." If he is gay, he may be thinking about his home too—his lover, and perhaps the new carpeting they are putting down in the living room. If he is interrupted, he becomes flustered and does not know what to say, or perhaps, adeptly, he says "I was thinking about the great chick I met last night." For gay people, internal gay worlds cannot be shared with straights in other worlds even in casual conversation, because the gay world is secret.

External time, divided by the calendar and by the clock, has the characteristic of what Lyman and Scott call "time tracks ... temporal periods employed by individuals, groups and whole cultures to designate the beginnings or the termination of things" (1970, p. 189). As they indicate, "time tracks are defined by events, activities, thoughts, or typifications of events, activities or thoughts, and movements from track to track may be marked by symbolism or rites of passage" (1970, p. 190). Time tracks are the external measurement of worlds.

Secret gay people often experience a kind of time schizophrenia. Time spent in worlds other than the straight one may be experienced both as unreal time and as split from the kind of time experienced in the gay world. The gay time track is leisure; the times spent at work, with one's family, and simply walking around the city have a different character and meaning for the gay person, since he can never externally "be himself" at these times. Gay time and leisure itself become of primary importance.

The split between gay and other times is a kind of splitting of the self, which can have emotional consequences for the gay person. Although some do not mind alternately wearing a mask and letting one's hair down (metaphors often used for the experience of self in straight and gay settings), others do. Whereas some do not mind relating to others dishonestly, fearfully, or impersonally in straight settings, others do. In either case, what might be one world is divided into two by stigma and secrecy, connected by tiny time tracks in which one self is exchanged for another:

> JOHN: You've got to be able to make instant changes—you can be flitting* around in one instant and just absolutely have to stop dead in the next. Uh—its like putting on a mask and taking it off and you have to

* Behaving in a camp, effeminate or flamboyant manner. See Chapter 5.

do it instantaneously you—and—literally you have to change your method of speech and everything else— your vocabulary changes—there's a lot of things that you would say in one instance that you would not say in the next, and you have to be able to turn it off and on just like you would a light switch. You get at home, you get in a leisure word—er leisure world after hours, and your vocabulary does change, you have a tendency to— to—socialize like the rest of the people do. (Tape-recorded interview)

For secret gay people, the only time they can really be themselves is in gay spaces, on the gay leisure world time track:

JEROME: You get into a gay bar, I think, it gives you a chance to—to really let your hair down, and say, you know, use the lingo, let the—you know, you don't have to put on any kind of a facade, because no one there is looking for you to be anything else but yourselves. (Tape-recorded interview)

The segmentation of time and space in this way is not a simple matter, however. Extreme secrecy and separation lie at one end of the continuum: openness and lack of concealment form the other:

Isadore, who is a wealthy married man, flies to another city in order to have sexual and social relationships with the gay community. (Anecdote)

ANTOINE: Everyone knows about me—how could they miss it. A hairdresser. Everyone at the salon knows too, but they don't say anything because they know if they did I would go somewhere else. My family knows too, and they are very good about it. I act the same everywhere. (Conversation)

Most gay people operate somewhere in between, sometimes easily, and sometimes most uncomfortably.

*Consciousness and Identity.*  Internal time, or consciousness, is vital in the search for identity characteristic of industrial society in general, and of those making the leap into a stigmatized community in particular. People about to make or break fundamental commitments to themselves or others, to answer the questions Who am I? and Where do I belong? in a way that will fatefully structure their lives, need time for reflection.

Consciousness and reflectivity are the essential psychic conditions for the building of an identity, just as space and external time tracks are the essential physical conditions. In quite different contexts, Merle Miller and Helen Merrill Lynd have given us insights into the relationship between states of consciousness and the growth of identity.

Writing on shame, Helen Lynd describes the experience of engaging in stigmatized behavior in terms of guilt and shame. Whereas guilt is a sense of responsibility to others, shame reflects responsibility to the self, and it is out of shame that a changed identity can come. In the act of feeling ashamed, the newly sexual adolescent—or the homosexually awakened adult—reflects upon the experience as a previously unknown possibility (Lynd, 1951).

Merle Miller, a novelist who came out publicly as a homosexual after years of secrecy, also discusses the importance of conscious reflection and of internal and divided time for the process of identity. In *On Being Different*, he indicates that when inner time becomes separated from outer time, the self is made aware that there is "something to hide" and opens to conscious exploration of what is being hidden and why. Ultimately, conscious reflection in inner time enables the development and taking of a homosexual identity. After this identity is assumed, the continuing division of inner and external time deepens the division between worlds and reinforces the sense of "being different" (Miller, 1971).

# 3. INTERACTION RITUAL

On the gay time track, in gay spaces, leisure is the major occupation of the gay community, the leisurely sociability that from another perspective is a kind of serious play. The secret gay world operates during leisure time, and the leisure that occupies the gay community takes highly ritualized forms that tend to pattern *all* leisure time.

Simmel, the analyst of secrecy, is also the theorist of sociability, which he describes as the play form of social interaction, whose goal is nothing but itself—play. The content of the play is talk, of the sociable conversation kind, in which "each individual should *offer* the maximum of sociable values (of joy, relief, liveliness, etc.) that is compatible with the maximum of values he himself receives" (Simmel, 1950, p. 47).

Talk of this kind is one element in gay sociability; the other is the correct setting. Whatever the spatial boundaries of the gay setting, and whatever the time of day, the setting must be adequately supplied with liquor (in some circles, on some occasions, wine or beer):

> JOHN: You're living in a very alcoholic society. Your whole social life is based on alcohol, because you always get together to talk to each other over cocktails. You always go out at night, and if you go to the bars you always drink to be sociable. There's very seldom that people get together and socialize over coffee. In this life, its always over cocktails.
> CAROL: Do you think that alcohol drinking is a problem in gay life?
> JOHN: No, I don't think so. I think its because of the attitude of the people, they've accepted the fact that the reason they drink is to be sociable, and—er—I think in any other form of life I would be an alcoholic now. I would have to be, as much as I drink, but I think my mental attitude is what prevents me from becoming an alcoholic—but I do it because—you know—what else is there to do in a bar? You feel almost literally uncomfortable in a bar, if you just sit there and smoke. I really can't explain why in this life 80 percent of us aren't alcoholics, as much as we drink—I think its just merely a form of relaxing your self between people, and not becoming a habit. (Tape-recorded interview)

In gay home sociability, a bargain is struck between hosts and guests. The hosts' obligation is to provide the liquor that will enable the guests to relax and engage in conversation; the guests' obligation is to do so, and to do so in a proper manner. If the liquor is insufficient, or if the talk is heavy, patchy, or too intimate instead of light, voluble, and witty, the sociable interaction is unsuccessful (Simmel, 1950, pp. 51–53).

Heavy talk is that dealing heavily with life or with heavy topics: talk about politics, religion, or philosophy, or sad tirades about love and death. When guests do engage in heavy talk, especially for a protracted time, the host may try to separate them or redirect the talk into anecdotal channels:

> Waxing philosophical, I pinned Simeon into a corner and went on for a while about the nature of love. After about five minutes he started fidgeting, and finally said, "Listen, don't you think that's a little heavy for a cocktail party?"

> The small group had been talking intensely for about half an hour. Jeremiah, the host, came up to them and said: "Come on, that's enough, break it up—you're supposed to be circulating." (Field notes)

Sociable talk is not heavy, nor is it intimate; heaviness suggests an overcommitment to the self, whereas intimacy suggests an overcommitment to the other, and neither is suitable for sociability:

> Jason and Richard sat on the sofa all through the party, alternately arguing and cuddling. After they left, Daryl said "Why don't those two just stay home if they want to carry on all night." (Field notes)

If intimacy is one pole of interaction, where the aim is simply knowledge of the other, business is the opposite pole, where the aim is independent of the other. Sociability, as play, is not compatible with either intimacy or business, and the doing of business at parties is also negatively sanctioned (Simmel, 1950, pp. 51–53).

> Sidney attempted to interest one of the guests in buying the product he sold for a living. Later, several people

commented that this display of salesmanship at a party
was "in bad taste." (Field notes)

Although the tone of sociable conversation is light, the
content is often anecdotal (Simmel, 1950, p. 53). In the gay
community, as in any other sociable setting, anecdotes
preserve the intimacy of the group by focusing on it, as well
as removing the talk from the intimacy of heaviness or love,
and from the impersonality of business. Anecdotes serve to
reinforce the solidarity, exclusiveness, and equality among
members of the community; their typical topics include
sexual liaisons, visits out of town and from out of towners,
bars, quarrels, presentations of self, and (although lightly) occupations:

> OLIVER: How are Jason and Richard getting along?
> LAUREN: Oh just fine, Jason has moved to Metropolis,
> and Richard is still living here, but they commute back
> and forth, and they're getting along better than ever . . . .

> NELSON: I saw Gino in the bar last night, and you
> should see what he picked up. A big black number with
> a shoulder bag. He didn't see me though . . .

> VIVA: You should really meet Harold and Bentley. We
> went up to their new home in Metropolis and its just
> gorgeous, we sat in the bathroom and had cocktails, it's
> enormous and all mirrored, with a sunken bath and
> purple carpets—
> CAROL: You sat in the bathroom?
> VIVA: Yes, its the only part of the house that's
> decorated yet, and they have the most *fabulous* gold
> Rolls Royce . . . .

> MARC: You should go to the new bar up on Eighth
> Street—they have a great drag show, and Tony the bar-
> tender that used to be at the Den five or six years ago is
> tending bar there . . . .

ALLAN: What's Dale doing now?
LARRY: Oh—he's working for some company up north.
Apparently he doesn't like it there—he misses Sun City.

JASON: . . . and then I had just had it with Bruce carrying on like that, getting so he fell in his plate. We had
spent hours on that dessert. So I just threw my glass at
him. It was full, too. Then I walked into the bedroom,
and shut the door. (Anecdotes; fragments)

There are certain types or patterns of sociability, that
occur in certain settings. The settings are either the public or
private spaces of the secret gay community; the types include routine home entertaining, cocktail parties, private
"spectaculars," public "spectaculars," and routine bargoing.
Each type of sociable interaction has a clear pattern, a legitimate number of participants, a time sequence, and a set of
rules of the game.

HOME ENTERTAINING. Routine home entertaining is the
mainstay of the middle-aged, middle-class secret gay community. Confined to leisure time, routine home entertaining
more usually takes place on weekends than on weekdays, in
the evening than in the day, and on Saturday than on Friday
or Sunday. The invitation may be for cocktails only, or, more
usually, for cocktails and dinner.

There are several defining characteristics of routine home
entertaining. First, the number of persons should neither be
so large that it becomes a full-scale party, nor as small as a
*tête-a-tête*; the usual number is from three to fifteen, or
twenty at a maximum. The ideal number is four to eight, and
fifteen is seen as pushing it:

Jeremiah, Olaf and another man gave a party in which
everything was just right: a lovely home, good food, lots

> to drink, and a congenial crowd of fourteen . . . . But that
> size crowd made talk quite difficult, since it was too
> large to make for general conversation, and too small
> for breaking into groups, especially in so large a house.
> The occasion was not a hit, as everyone, including the
> hosts, admitted later. (From field notes)

The second element, of course, is the ubiquitous liquor, but this defines all gay sociability, so it is not a hallmark of routine home entertaining. But liquor is a necessary element in making such entertainment "go," and the host, ensuring sociable conversation by his fulfillment of his obligation, never leaves a cocktail or wine glass (with dinner) empty throughout the evening. "Go," in fact, is partly dependent on the attainment of a degree of intoxication among the guests, as well as on the correct number of people.

The participants in routine home entertainment are either closer members of the gay community clique network (usually called "friends") or people the hosts particularly want to get to know. Thus the atmosphere of sociability in routine home entertaining verges upon the intimate pole of the spectrum rather than the cold, impersonal, and businesslike; sometimes even the norms against intimacy and heaviness are violated with impunity, but not often:

> Richard and Jason dined at Lauren's and Kim's house,
> and they all got into a deep discussion of occupations,
> relationships, and the gay community. Later, Richard
> announced: "I'm not going to their house for another six
> years. Its too much for me." (From field notes)

Heaviness or intimacy may be one reason a party does not "go"; sobriety of the guests can be another: this may be blamed either on the host's lack of adequate liquor provisions or on the guest's lack of conversational sociability:

> After Brian and Cyril left, Irving said: "Things really
> didn't go to well, did they?" I asked "Why did you say

that?" (although I knew; there had been an atmosphere of strain and silence rather than talkativeness and sociability), and he replied: "They hardly said a word all evening, and hardly loosened up at all. Maybe they had had a fight or something." Three days later when I saw Brian and Cyril I asked them how they liked the dinner. They both agreed that it didn't go very well, so they left early. I asked them why they thought it didn't go, and they said they really didn't know, it was just one of those evenings. (Field notes)

CAROL: Did you enjoy Darrell's last night?

JUSTIN: Yes, after dinner it really got going, but he served so fast people were just silent at first, but luckily he had wine.

(Later)

JUSTIN: Rollo gave us one drink before dinner. One drink.

JEREMIAH: I rattled and rattled my ice, but never got a refill.

ROLLO (laughs): What you didn't know was that I didn't have time to get to the store and get more, so I just ran out.

JEREMIAH: Next time I'm going to bring my own. (Conversations)

Although reasons can be found, the "go" of a party is difficult to reproduce in written form; it is a matter of atmosphere and comfort that have a far less tangible form than matters of liquor, conversation, and sponteneity. It is always clear whether a gathering has gone or not, but it is not always clear why.

The go of a cocktail party is even more important for the hosts than the go of routine home entertainment, since there is more investment (financially and otherwise) in a cocktail party, and the go is so much more publicized in the gay community grapevine. Because of the relatively great investment and risk, cocktail parties are much less frequent than routine home entertainment, taking place mainly on special occasions such as Christmas, Halloween, or perhaps a birthday:

> Guests begin to arrive about half an hour after the time specified on the invitation, and the first guests sit around uncomfortably with the hosts. During the next half hour the majority of the guests arrive, and, since the hosts have carefully removed all but a few chairs, people begin to stand and talk in groups.
>
> The first drinks are made by the hosts, who make sure that they are potent enough to get things going— they fill the tall glasses with ice, then two-thirds full of liquor, then add mix. After the greeting drink, guests make their own refills, which are frequent and also potent. The party begins to go within the first hour.
>
> People start to leave around 9, and all are gone by 10, many drunk. Whoever I asked within the next week about the party agreed that "It went really well—a very good party." (From field notes)

Although there are no exact rules for numbers of guests at a cocktail party, without at least fifteen or twenty the gathering becomes just a routine home entertainment. The top number I have seen at a cocktail party is around one hundred, the average is thirty to forty. Other designations that set cocktail parties off from routine entertainment are the sending of invitations, (sometimes) the luxury of the setting, and the special attention to dress.

Cocktail parties are most usually announced by invitation a month to two weeks preceding the event. The invitation specifies the time and place (usually a two-to three-hour period between 6 and 9:30 PM), and the dress, which may be casual, coat and tie or up to the guests. Again, the duty of the guests is to provide sociable conversation, while the task of the host is to provide enough liquor to get things going:

> Viva and Noreen have a wine punch to drink, which they ladle out of a large bowl. The twelve or so guests sit around quietly, and there are large gaps in the conversation. Most leave after half an hour or an hour.
>
> Jeremiah commented a few days later: "Really a bad deal over at Viva and Noreen's—punch will do it every time. Someday I'm going to tell them about it." (Field notes)

Occasionally the wealthiest members of the gay community will throw a cocktail party that by its extreme luxury qualifies as a spectacular. Although the hosts at any cocktail party add touches of luxury to the setting, and to themselves, for the occasion, the scale of luxury at spectaculars is far greater. Other telling characteristics of spectaculars are that they are large in scale, they are sometimes mixed rather than all-gay, and they may be formal or costume parties.

Few cocktail parties, and fewer routine home entertainments, mix straight and gay people to any degree. Spectaculars often do. In some cases the gathering is specified as a straight one, and although there may be a majority or sizable number of gay persons present, they are warned to "play straight." In other cases, the party is gay, with the straight persons warned beforehand:

> Two young gay males gave a black tie party specified as straight, for around three hundred people. According to one of the hosts, the party was about half gay and half straight, and ranged from gay unemployed to elderly, wealthy Sun City socialites. As the guests arrived, some were man-woman couples, others were alone, and still others were man-man and woman-woman couples. The party was outside in the warm

twilight, on several levels of patio. One level had been transformed into a dance floor with a band and a security guard to see that the guests did not fall over the cliff to the private beach below. Other levels contained the bars, an antique bathtub full of gin, and the buffet and dining tables, which were set in groups of six. The buffet table, topped by huge ice sculptures of swans, was laden with food and surrounded by banks of lilies, which also lined the pathways. The party began around 8 PM and ended in the early morning. Some of the gay members knew each other, and many gay tables were established for dinner.

The tone of the party remained straight throughout, and the event was written up next morning in the society column of the Sun City newspaper. However, an observer going from group to group could overhear snatches of gay conversation, and see some gay behavior. As one member commented, "At these affairs, water finds its own level."

Three older male homosexuals gave a costume party for about three hundred guests, the majority of whom were gay, and many of whom arrived in elaborate drag as showgirls and actresses. There was also a sizable minority of wise* straight people, including a well-known movie actress and a male singer famous in the 1950s. The house, garden and pool were lavishly decorated, and, since the promised band did not show up, music was piped through speakers. As guests entered, they gave their invitations to an off-duty policeman hired for the occasion, and paraded along a brightly lit pathway to the applause and comments of the crowd.

Drinks (inexpensive brands of liquor and mix) were poured by white-coated bartenders into plastic glasses, followed later in the evening by a buffet dinner and inexpensive champagne. Following dinner, there was a contest for the best costume. The winner was the most elaborate, worn by a close gay male friend of the hosts,

* See page 81.

and consisted of a skimpy costume of feathers, and a
sequined feather cloak, topped by a gigantic headdress
of feathers and sequins that measured at least five
feet, and kept swaying groundward. (Field notes)

My notes give an exactness to the definition of routine
home entertainment, cocktail parties, and spectaculars that in
most cases is there. Although there are ambiguously defined
social events in the gay community, most are clearly patterned and understood. A spectacular may be mixed, but it is
always large, lavish, and unusual; a cocktail party is sizable,
relatively unusual, and spans a short time period. Both are
announced by invitation. A routine home entertainment is
much more frequent, planned by telephone, and more
variable in size, intimacy, luxury, and content. The exact *point*
at which a gathering becomes a party or a party becomes a
spectacular in not exactly specifiable, but the types
themselves are most definitely so (see Simmel, 1950, pp.
111–113). The types are different, but they are all types of
sociability, since throughout them runs the twin themes of
light conversation and heavy drinking.

GAY BARS.   Unlike home entertainment, the interaction at
gay bars has two aims, either separate or together: sociability
and sexuality. This is not to say that men don't look for
sexual partners at parties; they do. But the aim of parties is
sociability; any sexual searching must be done fairly subtly,
since a man who hugs the walls silently and stares about will
not be as welcome at a party as he is in a bar. At some bars,
all the patrons are sociable, talking and laughing, whereas at
others nearly everyone is silent, looking around to catch the
eye of someone searching for a sex partner for the night.
Between home territory and cruising bars are many variations:

When Jason and I entered Christophers, there were
about fifteen people around the bar, engaged with the

bartender in one hilarious mass conversation. When we entered everyone fell silent, and stared at us. Within a few seconds the conversation had resumed, but we both felt very conspicuous.

Barbara's was jammed with men, many of them quite young. The music was so loud it was impossible to hear, and a few people were dancing. Most, however, were cruising—standing with their drinks, propped up against the wall, or leaning on the bar, looking around until they saw someone who caught their fancy, and who reciprocated by a meaningful look. As it reached 2 AM the looking became fairly frantic, as men who had come looking for a sex partner for the night still found themselves, at closing time, without one.

The Flyover is known as a friendly bar. Some groups are talking and laughing, while other men sit at the horseshoe shaped bar, or against the bar, looking around. Every now and then, one of the men alone is greeted by old friends, or approached by someone whose glance he has caught and held. (Field notes)

As Hooker comments, the essential feature of sexual searching in gay bars is "the standardized expectation that sex can be had without obligation or commitment" 1967, pp. 175–176).

Although sexual searching is often silent, sociability in bars, like home entertainment, is characterized by the reciprocal flow of liquor and conversation. Although the same rules of light talk obtain in a general way, the patrons have a greater flexibility of action than at a party, since they are buying their own liquor and are not obligated to any host. The varieties of bar behavior are much greater—friends may be lost in heavy conversation for hours, someone may feel unsociable and demand to be left alone to gloom over his beer, others chat and laugh.

In this instance, the liquor is provided by the management, so that it is in the management's interest to promote drinking, both for sociable and financial reasons. There are four main types of gay bars, with varying atmospheres and amenities: liquor bars, beer-and-wine bars, beer bars, and bars that serve only coffee and soft drinks or remain open after hours to serve coffee. The atmosphere and clientele often vary with the type of liquor license: the most elegant and smartest (and oldest) crowd at the liquor bars, the younger, more casual crowd at the beer and wine bars, and the youngest crowd when no alcoholic drinks are served:

> Midland's is decorated with a "movies" theme: posters of famous stars from silent pictures decorate the walls. There is a lot of gilt and plush: red booths and table-cloths with candles, red velvet curtains for the drag show, and crystal and gilt lights with cherubs all over the walls. Drinks are quite expensive, and there is a cover charge.

> The Hut serves beer only, and is described by its patrons as "a toilet." It is unusually grubby, and has no decor apart from a few mangy Mexican hats and bullfight posters on the wall. There is a juke box, a pool table, and assorted machines with games. A poster advertises hot sandwiches from a machine, and pitchers of beer are $1.50.

> The Cave just opened, to serve the college crowd. It is open to 18-year-olds because it serves only coffee and soft drinks. Its motif is psychedelic: black lights on posters, and a revolving circle of many colored lights on the dance floor. The place is clean and bare; the music from the juke box is so loud no one can hear anything, and the majority of the customers are on the large dance floor. (Field notes)

Cavan found in her study of (mostly straight) bar interaction that although there was pressure to drink something in bars, the drink need not be alcoholic (Cavan, 1965).

In many of the gay bars in Sun City, however, there is pressure to drink alcohol specifically, especially if the drinker is known to bartender or clientele. In liquor bars, furthermore, the patron may be pressured to drink cocktails rather than beer or wine:

> I went into Christophers and ordered a tonic. Jake, the bartender, said, in a questioning tone, *"Just* a tonic?" I reiterated my order. He said, "Feeling bad today? A gin and tonic would fix you up."

> Alvin bought Roland a drink, and Roland ordered a beer. Alvin said "Are you sure you wouldn't like something better? Maybe a Scotch?" Roland said, "Well, I have to get up early tomorrow and—but maybe I'll have a Scotch anyway."

Although the pressure may be overt or subtle, it is frequently there; it is the business of gay bars to purvey liquor, and the pleasure of the gay community to loosen tongues and inhibitions, both of which are accomplished best by drinking cocktails.

Getting drunk in gay bars, like getting drunk at home gatherings, is normal trouble in the gay community, rather than deviance. However, the community makes distinctions between drunkenness and normalcy on the one hand, and alcoholism on the other hand, just like the straight community, although perhaps with different definitions. Whereas alcoholism is drinking alone at home or getting drunk at every occasion of sociability, normal sociable drunkenness occurs only within groups and can be accounted for by the force of circumstances (such as being carried away by the extremes of sociability, being thrown over by a lover, or welcoming friends from out of town). Defined as alcoholism by the community is that drinking behavior which cannot be accounted for:

> OLIVER: I think Noreen has become an alcoholic. I saw her at the Flyover the other night, she was just stoned out of her mind.
> CAROL: I don't see that she drinks more than anyone else.
> OLIVER: Yes, but she is always stoned for no reason, and always *so* stoned. (Conversation)

Aside from sexual searching, which is a solitary activity,* there are several links between home-entertainment cliques and the bars. Some bars become home territories for cliques, and many are patronized by people who know each other on a regular basis. Bars are also used as a refuge from home entertainment, either from gatherings which have gone particularly well, or from gatherings which have not gone at all:

> The brunch started at 11 AM, so the guests arrived between 11:30 and 1:00 PM. People drank quite a lot of champagne, bloody marys and screwdrivers before food was served, which wasn't until 3:30. The last guests left around 6:00 PM, and by 6:30 most had extended their lively sociability to the local gay bar, where several stayed until the 2 AM closing time.

> Donald and Berger left almost immediately after dinner, which had been pleasant and quiet. "They always do that—I hate that," grumbled the host. "They always take off for the bars right after dinner. You really have to do a lot to entertain them." (Field notes)

Like home entertaining, the bars have special or spectacular occasions arranged by the management, usually on

---

* Except in the case where a couple is looking for a third partner. See Chapter 4 page 72.

special days like Valentine's Day, Halloween, and Easter, but sometimes just to attract customers. The major public spectacular occasion on the gay bar calender is Halloween, when the bars compete for patronage with private parties and with drag balls in rented hotel ballrooms. The forthcoming Halloween events are publicized mainly by poster and word of mouth, although there are written notices in gay publications:

> "Desmond" writes from "Sun City" that the Halloween festivities should be better than ever this year with two nights of fun and frolic in the area's twelve bars. On the Friday. . . there will be a buffet and prizes at (one bar). Then on the Saturday every bar will have something in the way of specials and prizes. . . . For those of you planning a forty-eight hour carnival, (another bar) will be open most of the night on Friday and Saturday. On Sunday. . . (they) will serve hearty brunches from 11 o'clock. So, if you're in the mood bring your wildest costume and plenty of stamina down to Sun City for Halloween. Remember, you are well treated and have no problems of any kind in this friendly city. (*California Scene*, 1970, p. 9).

The bars at Halloween are specially decorated, but the main event is getting into drag. Many customers (although not more than about a quarter at most Sun City bars) wear drag just to mingle, talk, and drink; in addition there is usually a drag contest at each bar. Sometimes different costumes compete; at other times the contestants rush breathlessly from bar to bar in the hope of winning more than one prize. Prizes can be as small as a bottle of champagne or as large as a trip to Hawaii. Winners are the most outrageous, spectacular, unusual, or costly drags, not the ones that best approximate females. Drag is intended as a spoof, not a replica, of female costuming:

I went around from bar to bar that Halloween. . . at Midlands, the drag contest had been held the night before. . . at the Furore, the bartenders wore skimpy velvet hotpants and cloaks. About one in ten of the customers were in drag, ranging from evening gowns to spoofs of pregnant sluts. A poster announced a drag contest to be held later that evening. . . . At Christophers, as usual, most of the patrons were at private parties, so it was quiet. A few men were in drag or modified drag—male clothes with makeup or a wig. . . .At Kenos the prizewinning costume, which won against replicas of Liza Minelli, or humorous versions of Laugh-In women, was a huge glittering butterfly. The man who wore it was young, and naked except for a small feather loin cloth and elaborate eye makeup and headdress. The rest of him was a huge and brilliant butterfly—wings of every color, covered with sequins and feathers. (Field notes)

DRUG USE. If drug use is defined as the use of psychoactive substances other than alcohol to change the nature of consciousness, there is some limited use of drugs in the gay community, although never in the sociable-ritual manner in which alcohol is used.* The only drugs I observed in sociable use were poppers (amyl nitrate) and marijuana. The private, sexual use of both of these was also reported to me, although the use of other drugs, such as heroin, pills, speed, or LSD, was not.

"Poppers" is a drug used recreationally and sexually in the gay community. Designed as a heart stimulant, poppers give a short-term, extreme high of five to ten minutes, characterized by euphoria and manic laughter over absolutely

---

* For a gay community in which drugs are used in this way, see Humphreys, 1972, p. 4.

nothing. It comes in large bottles or in small glass tubes which are broken under the nose, and it is inhaled. The substance is sometimes poured over the absorbent part of a nasal inhalant and used until it evaporates.

In Sun City, the legal status of poppers has fluctuated. In the late 1960s it was freely available in drugstores without prescription, and its use was common among a minority of the gay community. In the 1968–1970 period, the drug stores carrying the product grew increasingly reluctant to sell it, and eventually it was sold only on prescription. Although the many doctors of the gay community have access to the drug, its use has dropped off considerably. These examples are from 1968:

> There are about twenty people at the dinner party—half men and half women. All the men are gay, but some of the women are fag hags.* One of the fag hags, Noelle, is a famous TV and movie entertainer of the 1940s and 1950s. She has a box full of inhalers filled with amyl nitrate. She is drinking bourbon rapidly, and in between drinks she sniffs at an inhaler, sometimes leaving it stuck in her nose for quite a while. She is playing a dice game for quite high dollar stakes with some of the other guests, and frequently offers an inhalant to one of her fellow gamblers. Some accept, but they then start to refuse; then she slyly forces an inhalant up a nose when the person is not looking. Later, the hostesses commented on her excessive use of drugs and poor behavior.

> It is 4 AM, and despite the wishes of the seven men and three women, there are no more gay bars open. They are all quite drunk. They go to Alvin's house where they pour more drinks and Sven, who always carries amyl in an inhaler, passes it around the group. Everyone

* See Chapter 5, page 113.

laughs hysterically for some minutes every time it is
passed. It neutralizes, apparently, the effects of the alcohol, so people get soberer and soberer in between the
brief highs. Two of the men strip to their shorts and
dance around the room; when the high is over this
causes them considerable embarrassment, and they
hurry back into their clothes. People leave quickly,
sober, after that. (Field notes)

Reputedly more common than sociable use (and poppers
are not adaptable to light sociability) is the sexual use of the
substance. Amyl stimulates the heartbeat to several times its
normal rate and increases the intensity of orgasm if used
sexually.* Depending upon the sexual position used, the pop-
per is broken under the partner's nose just before orgasm, or
it is self-administered.

The use of poppers is not widespread, however, and is
seen as deviant by many members of the community when
used for sociability, probably because it destroys the lightness
characteristic of sociability. Marijuana, too, is used by some
groups in sociable settings (more often than poppers), but
this is also regarded as generally more suitable to sexual privacy and intimacy. The mood of quiet relaxation created by
the use of marijuana is less destructive to sociability than
poppers, but more so than the ubiquitous alcohol.

Because of the overlap between this gay community and
other, younger gay communities where marijuana and wine
have replaced scotch and cigarettes, there is some sociable
use of marijuana, although not in the ritualistic manner
characteristic of alcohol use. Some of the older community
members disapprove of marijuana use, and some will not
allow it in their homes, but its use most often creates an
uneasy tolerance:

---

* Given the hilarity induced by poppers, I find this hard to imagine, but I'm
told it is so.

> Several people are sitting around the pool, drinking bloody marys. Next to me, a group is passing around a marijuana cigarette. Samson, one of the hosts, tells them to stop; he doesn't approve of pot smoking, and they can do it in their home and not in his. They apologize, and put out the cigarette.
>
> About a month later at the party in their house, several people are smoking pot in the bedrooms. I ask Samson (who is in his mid-fifties) what he thinks of this, and he replies that there's nothing to do about it any more, everyone seems to be doing it. (Field notes)

> JASON: I took Richard over to Edward's house, and we all smoked pot and lay on the floor, and listened quietly to music. Next time I wanted to go there, Richard said he didn't want to go because it was a drag, so I went alone and he went to the bar, but he didn't like that either. (Conversation)

As these examples highlight, use of marijuana is most often found where this gay community intersects other gay communities and groups where marijuana use is accepted. Jason, for example, is nine years younger than his lover Richard, and much more ambivalent about his gay identity and about socializing with the gay community. He often prefers the company of young students like himself, who smoke grass and imagine themselves on the fringes of the counterculture. At Samson's house, too, the mix of ages, socioeconomic status, and gay clique affiliations is greater than normal, since Samson and his friend are eclectic in their invitations. In other gay cliques marijuana smoking is almost or completely unknown, at least for sociable purposes:

> OLIVER: Oh no, I never smoke grass except alone with a lover.
> CAROL: Aren't you concerned that it's illegal?
> OLIVER: So are all the other things I'm doing sweetie! (Conversation)

SOCIABILITY, STIGMA, AND SECRECY. A major characteristic of gay sociability is that it is deadly serious. Defining play as trivial is a mistake in any analysis of the gay world, since that play supports the most significant set of social relationships and meanings in the gay's environment. The traditional Puritan or Protestant ethic view of play is that it is both trivial and secondary to the world of work. Gay sociability, however, is work; it symbolizes both the centrality of leisure (since the secret gay world is a leisure one) and a "playful" nihilation of the straight world and all its seriousness.

Stigma, as well as secrecy, adds seriousness to gay play and takes seriousness from straight worlds of work and meaning. By stigmatizing the gay world the straight world sets gay people apart and releases some of society's power to control identity and community. Secrecy continues this differentiation, since straight society is never certain to whom it is talking.

As a result of seriousness, in the context of stigma and secrecy, those topics of sociability that occur in straight society may be left out of gay sociability, or they may be transformed beyond objective recognition. Although straight people often talk of work, occupations, education, and future plans (all serious, Protestant ethic things), gay people may not talk of these at all, or when they do, they play with the "seriousness" of these topics:

> When I told Alvin I was a sociologist he told me he had a degree in psychology from a famous university. Since he was a gardener and seemed to lack the ability to write even one sentence I doubted this, but did not question him. He lived in a beautiful house, and the situation called for a degree, so he produced one. The "truth" was irrelevant, and in any case unobtainable. (Field notes)

Other sociologists have asked me why I didn't get demographic data from my members: age, income, education, parents' income, and so on. The answer is that the content of sociability does not provide factual answers to these kinds of questions: demography is more likely to be used as just another aspect of the presentation of self.

Furthermore, the secrecy of the community and the danger-edged trust shared by the members prevent close scrutiny of work involvement and educational background (out of simple courtesy and tact, as well as the likelihood of being misled from the standpoint of cold sociological fact). These things are part of the *other* worlds gay people visit, and they are relevant in the gay world only as strategies of sociability. Like acres of white carpeting and a swimming pool, a degree and a job title are expressed luxuries of a given lifestyle:

> Viva and Noreen talked constantly of two "fabulous" men they knew who lived in a fantastic home and entertained a lot. When they one day visited the restaurant where one of them worked as a "dietician," he was actually a waiter. However, both he and they continued to describe him as a dietician. (Field notes)

Gay people are brought together as a stigmatized, secret group by sociability, and this is expressed in the way they greet one another. On entry to a dinner party, bar, or other gay setting, gay people kiss and hug one another fervently and warmly (although not with the intimacy of lovers), in a way which from the perspective of Puritanism might be called extravagant and flowery, particularly between two men. Even people who have known each other only a short while greet in this way; sometimes it spills over inadvertently into the straight world:

> Six or seven gay men entered the mixed party and began to kiss and hug the hosts and every gay man in sight. Quite drunk, they did not notice the surprised and

stiff El Sol matrons looking at them. Someone whispered "It's a mixed party, and the straights aren't wise," and they hurriedly stopped.

A gay man went to a straight party for his work colleagues, and had quite a bit to drink. At the door, without thinking, he reached over to give his host (of whom he was quite fond) a quick hug. The host drew back, astounded. (Field notes; anecdote)

The comparative analogy of the Puritan ethic and these occurrences of the mixing of worlds have been used to highlight the seriousness of gay sociable interaction, a playfulness that obscures the importance of it all if importance is seen as residing only in hard work, respectability, and guardedness. Moments of sociabililty and their expression in warm greeting, on the surface easy and light, have the poignancy of expressing the maskless identity of human beings, in the only setting where secrecy and stigma allow.

# 4. RELATIONSHIPS

In interaction, gay people experience different types of social relationship. Some members of the gay community are distant acquaintances, some are friends, some are lovers, and some are nameless strangers encountered once in a brief sexual act. Not just anyone, moreover, is considered eligible for a given type of relationship; like members of the straight world, gay people have social class, racial, ethnic, religious, and cosmetic stereotypes and prejudices which effectively limit their relationships with other members. Within the gay world there are two main types of social relationship: the clique relationship of sociability and the sexual relationship. The two are integrated by the long-term sexual relationship, which is the foundation of the clique system; like straight society, gay society is characterized by couple-oriented rather

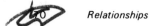 

*Relationships*

than single-oriented sociability. Sexual cruising in search of one-night stands, however, is more often accomplished alone.

Relationships with other gay people are fairly simple in outline, since the basis of everyone's identity, the core of his life, is known and understood in a way that makes for instant familiarity of at least a superficial sort, expressed in the physical warmth just described. Relationships with the straight world, for the secret community, are far more complex, since they involve the management of stigma and the concealment of the essential self even under conditions of friendly or familial intimacy.

SEXUALITY AND RELATIONSHIPS.  The core of stigma for the straight person is the homosexual act, and a gay person is one who prefers sexual acts with members of his own sex. This fact alone infuses short-term as well as long-term sexual affiliations with significance for identity. This does not seem true in the first ethnographic experiencing of the gay community, since the short-term relationship is almost completely outside the system of sociable community interaction and relationships; for example, some higher-status gay people prefer sexual contacts with lower-class men but confine their socialization to people like themselves. They "cruise" the lower-class bars for "rough trade"* and never integrate the partners they find into their sociable community interactions.

However, even this kind of short-term sexual relationship does have relevance for the maintenance of gay identity. First, cruising and its outcomes provide one of the bases for sociability itself—the telling of sexual anecdotes. Second, although these sexual encounters may not lead to intimacy or sociability, the members' awareness of belonging to a stig-

* Seek lower-class short-term sexual partners.

matized group is constantly sharpened by the reminder of the ultimate basis of that stigma—sexuality. Furthermore, even the most trivial, nameless, and superficial encounter with "trade" in a restroom is more real, in a sense, than the intimacy a secret gay has with family and straight friends, because with the other gay person he drops his mask of straightness and reveals his genuine self. In an important way, then, the married man who engages in tearoom trade* is sharing a significant side of himself with his casual sexual partner that is denied to wife and children, and even the community-oriented gay demonstrates the basis of his fundamental allegiances in his sexuality—an allegiance, as Simmel points out, not given to parents, workmates, or old high school buddies (1950, p. 369).

Whereas the short-term sexual relationship has singular relevance for gay identity but little for community, the *long-term sexual relationship* is vital for the maintenance of community. Gay community sociability, like straight partying, is more a couple-oriented than a single phenomenon, although there are many singles in established gay circles too. The partners in a long-term sexual relationship are generally referred to as "lovers," and sometimes "friends" or "partners." Their relationship is sometimes described as "marriage," a term which is also used with heterosexual marriages. More recently, another meaning has been added—gay marriage-ceremony marriage, which of course is rare in the secret community. This triple usage can lead to confusion:

> Viva and Rachel sent out party invitations inscribed "in honor of the marriage of Viva and Rachel." The "crowd" speculated about this, wondering if they were actually going to have a ceremony, and clucking tongues over "how terrible that would be." Viva and Rachel

* Oral sexual activity which takes place in restrooms. See Humphreys, 1970.

> played along, claiming they were to be married by a
> gay Black Muslim. Of course, when the night of the
> party arrived there was no such ceremony.
>
> The same interrogation was repeated with each new ar-
> rival "Do you know Arno? He's getting married." Most
> people asked "To a girl?" while some made assump-
> tions in both directions, and still others asked "What do
> you mean?" or "What kind of married?" (Field notes)

There are three models of long-term sexual relationship or
marriage within the community: a faithful marriage modeled
on that of heterosexual couples, a marriage with an open "arrangement," and a marriage with a three-way arrangement.
The "heterosexual monogamous" marriage is regarded as im-
practical—at best a stage at the beginning of a long-term
sexual relationship, to be superseded by one of the other
"more realistic and mature" types. Fidelity between two
males is regarded as even more unnatural and unenforceable
than fidelity between man and woman or between two
women. Many men attribute the demise of so many gay
womens' relationships to the attempt by women to ensure
partner fidelity. From this, they argue, ensue secret affairs,
jealousy, scenes, and breakups. "Arrangements" are seen as
a far better option:

> REEVES (at a party): See that guy over there? What's
> his name?
> CAROL: Bartlett.
> REEVES: I was with him in the baths the other day, he
> goes there and so does his friend, but each of them
> pretends he doesn't go and doesn't know about the
> other one. It's so dumb. Me and Derek, we are more
> honest with each other.

In the open type of arrangement, partners are free to seek
casual short-term relationships with other men; the accent is

on both "casual" and "short-term." Like heterosexual "swingers," gay lovers are well aware of the dangers to a love relationship of emotional or long-term involvement with someone else:

> PATTERSON: We go with different people, as long as it's only one night stands. Longer than that, there are problems.
>
> CAROL: Have you ever had these kinds of problems?
>
> PATTERSON: Yes. One time when Emil was away I met this kid, and we really got hot and heavy. Emil flew back and I broke it off—it wasn't easy. Since then we decided on the one night stand rule. Only that one time.
>
> CAROL: Do you still have sex with each other?
>
> PATTERSON: Yes, most of the time. The only time I really go out* is when Emil is away, and other than that probably not more than once a month, if that.
>
> CAROL: When did that start, and how?
>
> PATTERSON: What do you mean?
>
> CAROL: I mean, did you make a conscious decision, or. . . .
>
> PATTERSON: Oh no. We were together about a year, then we both started going out. We never talked about it, that was just the way it was. (Conversation)

In a three-way arrangement, which is common, the partners are not free to seek casual sex outside the partnership; together, the lovers seek sex with another individual in a three-way (sometimes four-way, or orgy) sexual experience:

> JOHN: Maybe they consider the fact that they're still being faithful to each other as long as they do not individually go out with another person, as long as the other person is involved, then their relationship seems

---

* The expression "to go out" is often used as a euphemism for sex, especially of this type.

to stand very evenly. I mean, an awful lot of people do this, and of the people that I know that do this I can't think of one of them in any conversation or even talking to anybody else would think of going out with that person alone. It's always "my partner and I"—I think it's the fact that they're still involving one another, they're not excluding the other person.

CAROL: And this is more frequent than, say, each person going out with another person?

JOHN: I think so, especially if the relationship is lasting or going to—has the appearance of lasting.

CAROL: Do you think there are many relationships in which faithfulness is practiced, as well as preached?

JOHN: I think so—uh—(pause)—I don't know what the percentage would be—it's hard to even guess at the percentage in this, but I wouldn't say an awful lot of them, because there aren't that many marriages that seem to last for any length of time. So many people stay together for nine or ten years and then break up over something—after that length of time you generally end up with houses and cars and property and everything else that's in both people's names so it's pretty hard to break something like that up. Besides that, by the time you're at an older age bracket, and you're not—you've got something, or somebody, and you become accustomed to them, and other than getting in on this three-way bit—I know a few of them it is just permanent between the two of them, they don't go out and romp and tromp with other people. (Tape-recorded interview)

Unlike the open arrangement, those eligible for a three-way may be strangers or long-term friends, since, in gay folklore, when both partners are present during sex, emotional involvement with the third poses no threat to the relationship:

NEVILLE: Thomas is coming to stay—he was our third when we lived in Seattle, and then whenever he came

to Sun City. He wrote us that he's got a new lover now,
so he just wants to visit this time. (Conversation)

Eligibility for a short-term sexual relationship is based on
different criteria than eligibility for a long-term relationship, or
for friendship. Like the majority of American society, gay men
select their lovers according to general rules of ethnic, racial,
age, and class similarity, although there are exceptions. The
short-term sexual relationship, on the other hand, is based
more on strictly sexual preferences; the partner may be
white, middle-class, and in his thirties, but the preferred
stranger could be black, lower-class, and very young. Jason
expressed the dilemma of an individual who prefers lower-
class men sexually but is seeking a long-term relationship
with someone of the same (professional) class:

> My trouble is, I prefer sexually rather lower-class men,
> so I go to funky lower-class bars to find them. But I
> couldn't make a life with someone like that, so I want to
> find someone of my own general occupation—but they
> never seem to appeal to me sexually. (Conversation)

In most cliques, the norm is that the members find short-
term sexual relationships outside the group, either among
strangers in bars or from connected cliques. In some groups
this proscriptive rule amounts to an incest taboo; candidates
for short-term sex must be found among strangers or at best
acquaintances, and not among roommates, friends, or lovers.
Even the explanations for this are reminiscent of explanations
given by sociologists for the existence of the incest taboo:

> CAROL: If you were feeling sexy, would you turn to
> either one of these two (friend and roommate) or would
> you go to a bar to see who you could pick up—just for
> sex?
> LONNY: I'd sooner go to a bar.
> CAROL: Why do you think this is?

> LONNY: Sexually, I don't think they would satisfy me.
>
> CAROL: Why do you think this?
>
> LONNY: No, one of them, yes, would satisfy me, but with a sexual act you have to have—or you should have I think—I'm not sure—an attractive—how can I put it?—sexual drive with an eye between an eye or a look between a look—and then it adds to it—and you're pushed by yourself to continue the act. With the latter two—um—I'd probably go to bed and go to sleep. (Tape-recorded interview)

In a minority of groups this taboo is not observed:

> BARRY: I looked around the group the other day and thought, talk about musical beds, everyone has been with everyone, people just sort of trade off. Must be because this is such a small town (a beach town close to Sun City).

In other cases, individuals would prefer that it didn't:

> JASON: In the gay world, I don't understand it, people would rather have sex with a stranger than a friend. I would rather turn to someone I knew. (Conversations)

SOCIABILITY AND RELATIONSHIPS.  Sociability is the main activity of the gay community, engaged in by singles and by couples who are in long-term sexual relationships. These couples, in turn, socialize with others (chosen by various criteria of race, ethnicity, social class, and age) in sociable relationships. Unlike sexuality, which is generally between two or three,* sociable relationships involve numbers of people from two or three upward to the hundreds.

* By repute, orgies are rare.

The main group sustaining community interaction is the *clique*, and the form of relationship between clique members is the *relationship of obligation*. The obligation is to provide the highly ritualized occasions of sociability for co-members, as described in the previous chapter:

> JASON: You tend to meet people through friends—who are interested in introducing friends to friends who don't know each other. And that happens sometimes, it happens really quite often, although—um—it seems like that when you travel in confined circles, you know, in people's homes for dinner and brunch and so forth, er— it may very quickly—becomes a very closed kind of crowd, and although you may initially meet some new faces, you don't continue to meet many new faces and it always seems like because of circumstances—um— you know—the new faces that you meet through private circles aren't the people that you get involved with—I suppose the most usual thing is that you meet people, and through a series of circumstances you keep meeting them, and you become involved in a relationship of obligation in the sense that they've had you to their house, and you've had them to yours, and the reciprocal invitation is—has to be made, out of politeness, and a lot of the—er—the private circles and so forth seem to be made up primarily of people who are, you know, obligated to each other in terms of some kind of etiquette, and the continual dynamics of that sort of scene, you know, get played out, because of the obligations which have to be met, and people aren't involved with each other really either on a short-term sexual basis nor as—you know—really good friends, nor as even long term sexual partners, but it's, it's kind of a thing where you have acquaintances, and, well, you know, you know—people, and you have obligations to people so you invite them or they invite you out in turn, and the whole thing keeps on going. So the outcome—

the most typical outcome that I see is a relationship of
obligation rather than a relationship of friendship or one
of short-term or long-term sex. (Tape-recorded interview)

The interaction which sustains the relationship of obligation, as indicated in the previous chapter, is highly ritualized, patterned, and normative: cocktail parties, dinner
parties, and cocktail get-togethers, sustained by the mutual
expectation of host and guest to provide liquor for sociable
talk. The relationship of obligation itself, too, involves highly
ritualized, patterned, and normative performances of obligation, and sets up mutual expectations of sociability. For
example, the acceptance of a dinner party invitation by a
couple or single involves the implicit acceptance to give a reciprocal entertainment at a later date. Similarly, a cocktail
get-together involves the implied acceptance of the obligation to give a reciprocal or greater (dinner party) obligation.
The accent is on equal or greater returns of obligation: a
cocktail get-together is not an adequate return for a dinner
party, although a brunch is.

Although clique members entertain each other in this way,
there is always room for new members since cliques tend
generally to be in a state of flux. The entertainment of a
new single or couple involves them in an obligation of
politeness to give one reciprocal entertainment; if the matter
is not taken up again, the relationship may be dropped. With
the third contact, a relationship of obligation is set in motion.

Cocktail parties and spectaculars, which draw on larger
numbers than routine home entertainment, require that
people other than clique members be invited. List-making for
such a party is interesting to observe: first, the current clique
members are listed, then acquaintances who are routinely
invited to larger parties but never to more intimate gatherings, then couples who have been dropped as clique
members, members of overlapping cliques, out of towners,

and people the hosts have just met. Cliques that never otherwise coincide meet at this kind of party:

> I knew most of the people at the party. There were the
> members of the three cliques to which Aaron and
> Manfred belonged, but who rarely saw each other
> anywhere else. I asked Aaron to account for the faces I
> did not know: "Will and Bob just got into town from
> LA—they're living in Blue Waters—real nice guys—
> then there's Fred, we used to see a lot of him when he
> was with Alan, but we don't see much of him now. That
> guy over there Manfred just dragged in from the bars, I
> really don't know who he is, and I'm about to find out"
> (laughter). (Field notes)

Because they are so socially promiscuous, parties of this
kind do not fulfill standing obligations for dinner parties by
co-clique members, and people invited to a cocktail party are
not expected to give one in return (although if they do they
are obligated to ask the hosts of those they have at-
tended). Perhaps because of this, cocktail parties are infre-
quent and occasional (in both senses of the term), since they
involve a considerable expense for which very little return
can be expected, in either fulfilling obligations or generating
new ones.

Clique members are aware, for each different size and style
of clique, of the amount of time which can be allowed to
elapse between entertainments. There is no general norm in
the community, but members who are lax in understanding
and fulfilling the obligations they take on with group
membership are sanctioned:

> JUSTIN: Viva and Noreen are just terrible; they haven't
> invited any of us over for ages, and Darrell and Francis
> have had them over six or seven times for dinner. I
> wouldn't do it; I won't ask them again till they have me
> over. (Conversation)

The nuances of relationships of obligation are a strange mixture of precision and vagueness, depending on the members' gradual socialization into, empathy with, and desire for acceptance in the gay community. When all three are high, the person becomes a master at socializing and fulfilling obligations; when they are low, he risks being defined as an inept bungler, or perhaps outside the pale of social acceptability entirely. Among the nuances: more than one couple or single co-clique member may be invited to an entertainment which fulfills obligations, but not too many of them or it becomes a party and "doesn't count"; certain persons are by common agreement exempt from returning obligations,* but this applies to very few persons; small cliques allow less time to elapse between entertainments than large ones; declining invitations more than once constitutes a rejection of sociability overtures; and mixing straight and gay people is in most cases very bad form, unless the host has checked it out with all the gay guests first. This nuance, of course, is a protective norm in a secret and stigmatized society.

CLASS AND CASTE IN THE GAY WORLD.    In any community the members use criteria for sorting persons into suitability categories for forming relationships—sexual, sociable, and others. In the gay community, there are two levels of criteria: membership in the gay world itself, and, within that membership, criteria specifying who is accessible or legitimate as a sexual, sociable, friendly, or other type of relational partner.

Most members of this gay community are gay males; however, although secret and stigmatized societies generally

---

* The two men I met (Owen and Horace) who were apparently exempt from returning obligations were both single, academics, fairly well off, very well liked, and quite individualistic. Aside from these personality features, I could distinguish no reasons for their exemption.

exclude persons who do not share the stigma,* there is a small minority of members who are straight, or women, or both straight and female. The membership of women in gay men's groups serves functions for both the men and the women. The men cite such things as the attractiveness of the women as decorative objects at parties in the gay world; many also like to try on their earrings, tell them how to dress, and so on. The heterosexual women, many of whom are divorced and some of whom are middle aged, get attention from the gay community without commitment or sexual threat. The gay women are most often those who do not fit into the lesbian community: they may be professional in occupation, prefer more traditionally "feminine" dress than the norm in the lesbian community, or prefer the company of men. Many of the women state that the gay men are polite and gentlemanly, and reinforce their femininity. For both the gay men and the gay women, the opposite sex may be used to construct a front in the straight world, for family or workmates.

Some cliques, of course, are all-male, and a few of these would not admit women under any circumstances. But most cliques have at least one of the following kinds of member or acquaintance: homosexual female, heterosexual female, heterosexual married couple, or heterosexual male, in that order of likelihood (I personally observed no cases of cliques with, or acquainted with heterosexual males, but I have heard of a few instances). Heterosexual members of gay groups must, of course, be "wise" † and accepting of the gay scene, and enjoy interaction with a gay theme.

Beyond the overriding criterion of membership in the gay world or "wise" courtesy membership, membership in the specific cliques is stratified by caste and social class. The

* For example, "swingers" generally exclude nonswingers from their parties.
† A "wise" straight person is one who knows about and does not stigmatize the gay community. See also Goffman, 1963.

class criteria within the gay community have the same elements of occupational prestige, income, and education as in the straight world, with some specifically gay values added. The members are aware of the implications of social class in their world, and give classes names: upper or "elite," middle or "career," and lower or "deviant":

> JOHN: Well, basically I think you can categorize gay kids the same as you can any other social environment, religion for instance. Because you have—er—low trashy type people that I feel consist of the cruisers, you know, on the streets, um, possible deviants that do prey on younger children, and then you have business people that are really trying to make something out of their life. . . . We're living in a double standard of society, because I'm living in one and other people are living in another, and you also have classes within that society. You put yourself on your social level within that particular group and the majority of people that you meet are on your same level and plane, and when you do see them you're not worried about it. Now if I ran into some of the people that I have a nodding acquaintance with in a bar—er—granted, I might have a tendency to get a little panicky at times because it wouldn't surprise me in the least if they ran up to you and threw their arms around you in broad daylight down on Broadway, you know, and you're walking down the street with three or four business acquaintances. . . . Well, what do you do in a situation like this? (laughs). But again—er—they are generally associating with people in this particular society that they enjoy and that their particular mental capabilities seem to go along with, and you are generally in your own element . . . it's no different from separating the people who live in (low-rent district) from the ones that live in (high rent-district). (Tape-recorded interview)

> CAROL: Do you think there's more than one kind of gay circle?

SEBASTIAN: Oh most definitely yes.

CAROL: What kinds are there?

SEBASTIAN: Well, you go all the way from the low class, the real trash . . . to the very elegant people. . . . I have so many different types of gay friends that sometimes I have to be what one would term very prissy, very elegant, and very pulled-together. . . . I usually only associate, I mean, my friends—gay friends like myself; we, er, work very hard for a living, and conform pretty much to what society dictates . . . then there are the other ones . . . drag queens, who live in drag all the time, uh, male prostitutes, and, er, people who don't—who aren't very aware of where they're going, or what they want or what they can get out of life if they really tried, through education and travel, and er, want of the finer things of life.

CAROL: How many of these levels would you say there are?

SEBASTIAN: How many levels: Well, let's see—there is the low class, middle class, and high class.

CAROL: Is this true in the gay world, do you think?

SEBASTIAN: Oh, I think so. Yes, certainly. And I know people from all levels.

As these comments indicate, the members see the social class "structure" of their community in many of the same terms that sociologists view social class: the elite or upper class encompasses those men and women of higher (business and professional) and stable occupational status, who are concerned with their occupational careers, who conform to traditional norms of conduct, dress, and materialistic values, who are of "higher educational and intelligence" levels, and who live in the better parts of town. Similarly, the middle or career class* is unstable occupationally, has less education, and has a more casual lifestyle.

* Use this term because the members' gayness itself, and their leisure pursuits, literally become their career.

The gay world adds its own criteria to this scheme, however. Elite class members are elegantly dressed and have an elegant lifestyle, whereas career gays are free to join gay liberation, act effeminate or outrageous, and flout convention. The lower class is a residual category into which the elite and career put a variety of troublesome deviants[†]: transvestites, child molesters, male prostitutes, and others.

My observations confirmed what the members said about the social class element of clique formation and socialization. Elite cliques contain middle-aged (for the gay world: late twenties through senior citizenship) men in various stable occupations in business and the professions. Although many of them do socialize in bars, most of their contacts take place in private homes. Many own their own homes and have a stable long-term relationship with another man.

The career class is a younger group, early twenties, and even teens, to thirties, who transmit a large amount of their life energy into being gay; they do not have stable occupations, and often spend "normal working hours" as well as leisure hours cruising in the bars. They rent their places of residence; both their homes and their sexual and roommate partnerships are unstable. Their clique relationships are usually drinking partnerships, which are often quite stable over time. The deviant or lower class (of which I have very little personal observational data) is a residual category into which is typed those who appear unacceptable to elite or career groups (see Leznoff and Westley, 1967).

The members' model of social class in their world is quite abstract and tends to be only partially borne out in interaction, which is much more fluid—as Sebastian said, he had all kinds of friends. Although many cliques are completely closed to outsiders, just as many are permeable by a

[†] See Chapter 6 for a discussion of the members' use of the term "deviant."

member of another "class," especially if he happens to be very good looking (the only infallible trans-class passport in the gay world):

> CAROL: Do you think that there's much class mixing within the gay community?
> JOHN: Some, not much. Er—well, that's kind of hard to say, because I think that its—there is a lot of it really, and I would say basically it's done at large parties which I have been to . . . but not so much if you're in a particular social group; they have—do not have a tendency to invite people outside of that particular area. (Tape-recorded interview)

Why this (typical) confusion between the abstract class model and actual interaction? First, it is clear that members tend to think of themselves, no matter what the abstract criteria, as members of the elite class (nearly all my respondents did, and I would agree with about two-thirds of them). This appears to be for the sorts of reasons mentioned in the previous chapter: since an elegant upper-middle-class lifestyle is one of the status hallmarks of the gay community, it is quite difficult to tell, and especially in the context of secrecy, what socioeconomic status people actually have. Even those members who do not have a prestige occupation, a good income, and a high level of education act as if they do, or learn to act as if they do. Similarly, it is preferable to have friends of a high status; thus people are willing to suspend disbelief in the status of others, as well as embellish their own. John's confusion over whether there is class mixing is a function of this type of confusion of levels of meaning, from objective (unobservable) fact to playful invention.

Although most of my respondents defined themselves as members of the elite class of the gay community, a few did not. One of the exceptions was Simeon, who claimed that he was moving socially from career to elite status because of the prestige of his new lover—and without actual change in occupation, education, or income:

> CAROL: Before you got together with your present friend, did you do as much home socializing, or did you go out to the bars?
>
> SIMEON: No—I did as much—I started to say no—because I've met an entirely different crowd and don't see any of my older friends, but I—went to homes—I go to homes more than I thought I did now that I think about it. For instance, when I lived next door to the stripper and her friend I was in their home all the time and I'd classify that as a home visit, although really it was my own home—we were just twenty feet apart.
>
> CAROL: Do you think—when you say a different type of people, what do you mean?
>
> SIMEON: Well, the old crowd was hairdressers, strippers and god knows what, and the new crowd is a much better crowd—its'—bartenders, hairdressers and strippers (laughs).
>
> CAROL: It doesn't sound very different.
>
> SIMEON: No—but they're a different type of people—mainly the individuals that make up the crowd, that's what it is.
>
> CAROL: I know it's individuals, but what kind of differences are there?
>
> SIMEON: The way they live, their background, their educational background especially—of course I tend to put that to my lover's credit, its just that we've stopped seeing my old crowd which was kind of a toilet group, and have fallen in with a new crowd, which is not so much so.
>
> CAROL: Well, what's the differences? What do you think the essential differences are?
>
> SIMEON: Well, for instance, a lot of the old crowd

didn't have steady jobs and wasn't interested in getting one. That's one reason I didn't get anywhere on my job for so long.\* It was because most of my friends didn't have a job and I thought I was doing well just to have a job, and I didn't consider to advance myself. When I finally got a spur up too I got a promotion in what—a month and a half's time.

CAROL: Which crowd do you prefer?

SIMEON: I prefer this one really. In fact, I avoid the old one when out in public now, which is sometimes impossible to do.

CAROL: Are there any in the new crowd that have different kinds of occupation?

SIMEON: Well, actually the new crowd is still small, and is centered, of course around my lover and myself. One guy owns the bar, another guy is the bartender, and his lover is actually unemployed, and I don't know what he did. And my roommate was working for the airlines when I met him. God, that sounds really meager, doesn't it? They're all connected with the bar.

CAROL: And—give your lover's occupation, the general category—

SIMEON: Social work.

CAROL: But none of your crowd is in that kind of occupational group category apart from your lover?

SIMEON: Not really—some of his friends who aren't really my friends yet are—people who I've just met.

Clearly, there are some people in the community about whom I, or any other observer, have factual knowledge with reference to occupational criteria; but there are many more where the only available knowlege is phenomenological,

---

\* A night watchman. He could visit the bars all day and also after he got off work for the last hour of cruising, from 1 to 2 AM.

suited to the purpose of the member at the time. Just as Simeon's knowledge of the occupations of persons close to him—strippers, bartenders, hairdressers, and unemployed—is probably accurate, my knowledge of the occupations of some of the members was based on close acquaintanceship or observation. For the majority of persons, however, both of us know only what it was thought best for us to know: a teacher might pose as a hairdresser to preserve secrecy; a hairdresser would claim to be a salon owner to gain prestige; and a welfare worker might state that he headed the whole county organization for the same kinds of reason.

Caste divisions, particularly black-white differentiation, tend to be even more clear-cut in the gay community than social class divisions, since unlike the questions of class, people cannot hide or elaborate on their skin color. In my research I met only a few community members who were not "Anglo": one black man with a white lover, one black woman with a white lover, and a few American Indians and Orientals. Communities are structured along ethnic lines in the gay world: there are all-black communities, all-Chicano communities, and communities composed only of interracial gay couples.

Of course, this generalization is in the area of sociability and relationships of obligation. There were many instances in which white members talked about or were seen to have short-term sexual relationships with blacks or other minority group members; indeed, some gay people were described as having sexual "hang ups" directed toward blacks, Orientals, Chicanos, or others. But, like the caste system in the southern United States during slavery and after, sexual use, for many, did not extend to social acceptability or long-term sexuality and affection.

The ideological statements about class and caste by gays give a very different picture:

CAROL: Do you think there's much race mixing in the gay life?

JOHN: Not too much—oh you mean—mixture—of no barriers between them? Oh yeah, people just don't care. (Tape-recorded interview)

Donald Webster Cory, like many other gay legitimators, remarks:

The deep-rooted prejudices that restrict marriages and friendships according to social strata—family, wealth, religion, color, and a myriad of other artifices—are conspicuously absent among the submerged groups that make up the homosexual society. (Cory, 1950, p. 53)

Again, why the disparity between ideology and observed practice? One reason is that gay identity is a master status for those who commit themselves to the secret community; it is the most important and defining characteristic of the members' selves. But once this basic identity criterion is established, in this community at least, most members tend to select their friends, acquaintances, and lovers according to the usual caste and class prejudices of American society.

On the other hand, the overriding gay identity criterion can neutralize prejudice where there is some sort of conflict; thus a traveling gay, faced with a choice of companions on a charter flight, will choose a black gay couple rather than a white straight couple, although at home he may have no minority group friends. And the following conversation is from an individual who generally expresses "racist" sentiments when discussing issues of law and order, welfare, and so on:

JEREMIAH: I am sick of the colored people the way they are today, getting something for nothing.

CAROL: What about gay black people?
JEREMIAH: I don't know any personally, but I'm sure they would be like the rest of us, we work hard for a living and don't riot and go on welfare.

FRIENDSHIP.   As Simmel indicates, the thresholds of sociability are friendship and business. With regard to friendship, interaction has as its purpose not just play but intimacy—the sharing of a deeply felt personal relationship (Simmel, 1950, pp. 46–47). Members of the gay community generally refer to their clique acquaintances as "friends," but on the other hand they distinguish between "real friendship" and relationships of obligation, which may overlap:

JUSTIN: I went to see Alice in the hospital, she's having a cancer operation.
CAROL: I didn't realize you saw her any more.
JUSTIN: I don't. I haven't seen her in over a year—and she lives just down the road.
CAROL: Then why are you going to see her?
JUSTIN: Well, she's a real friend—for years—although I wouldn't see her much now because of the crowd I run with now, they wouldn't like that type of person. She's a friend from an earlier time, but a friend. (Conversation)

CAROL: Do you think that the friendships in the gay world are—from your experience—the friendships you've had with gay people, are they as lasting as the friendships you've had with straight people?
JOHN: I don't think so. Uh—think there's a lot of angles on that—first of all because gay people notoriously move around a lot so that you know people for brief periods of time, and you don't have a chance to know them for extended periods of time—uh—they're much more chummy about their relationships with each

other—you know—when they run into each other if
they haven't seen each other for a while you'd think
they were running into their long-lost best friend in the
world. I mean, even if you've known someone for a
year, the friendships are very instantaneous generally—
er—first of all because they don't have time to mature,
and you can't nurture them over a period of years.
(Tape-recorded interview)

Oliver had a friend Simeon for many years. Unlike
Oliver, Simeon was of a lower status occupation, and
interacted with cliques of bartenders and strippers,
while Oliver's clique was mostly professional people.
They went to different parties, different gay bars, and
had no relationships of obligation in common. Yet they
defined themselves as "best friends"—had long talks
into the night, cried on each other's shoulders, and
generally depended on one another for intimacy and
warmth. (Summarized from field notes)

As these examples show, "real friends" may be either
straight or gay, and inside or outside the relationships of obli-
gaton. Indeed, gayness and membership in sociability cliques
may be more barriers to friendship than inducements, for
several reasons. For one thing, as John points out, gay people
"move around a lot," which can have an effect on friendship,
if indirectly. American society is highly mobile, and gays are
not the only people who move around; however, when they
do move, they can easily meet and become integrated into a
ready-made circle of gays, in a way the nonstigmatized may
not, and thus not depend for friendship or fun on "keeping up
with" old friends. Furthermore, the superficial intimacy of the
relationship of obligation, as John points out, can preclude
the development of a real intimacy.

"Real friends" who are straight are probably the only
persons in a secret gay's life who share the secret but not the

stigma—which gives them a special character. It is no feat to share life and identity with another gay person; it is one to share with a straight person who is accepting and intimate. Although some gays who have straight friends claim that the friends "do not know," most of the community agrees that if a straight is to be a friend, he or she *must* share the secret that is the basis of gay identity. The friends must either be told or have an unspoken understanding.

Two types of straight people may share a gay person's secret world: intimate friends, who generally confine their knowledge and association to the particular gay person, and wise straight people who are part of the sociable gay community. One group of straights who rarely enter the secret world is the gay's family of origin. Although most people had told some straight friends about their gayness, few had ever told parents or siblings; of those who had, most told mothers, and for the family the matter often remained a closed issue anyway. In many instances, parents who were told or who found out about their offspring's gayness simply ignored the whole thing and never mentioned it again. This was generally acceptable in the secret gay community; the overt community, however, has developed compensatory tactics to force the parents to recognize gayness as an issue. One of these is inviting the entire family to dinner at a gay restaurant, and then making the announcement. There are exceptions to all these rules:

> At the gay motel I observed a man (who clearly had on some light makeup) in his late twenties accompanied by a woman in her forties or fifties, and an elderly woman in her seventies. Upon inquiry, I found out that they were his mother and grandmother. I cornered him by the pool and squeezed some information out of him, although it was quickly apparent that he wasn't too keen on females:

ROBERT: Yes, that's my mother and grandmother. My mother was at Deep Sea Dick's last night (a gay bar) and had a great time. I was dancing with Peter.

CAROL: Was your grandmother there?

ROBERT: No, just my mother.

CAROL: How does she accept it?

ROBERT: Oh, just fine—she's always talking about the gay scene, asking is he gay, and so on—she's very interested.

CAROL: How about your grandmother?

ROBERT: It was more difficult for her to accept. But she finally did. But she doesn't talk about it.

CAROL: What made you tell them?

ROBERT: I didn't. My ex-wife found out about it, and she wrote a letter to all my family.*

CAROL: What did they say?

ROBERT: My mother said, I probably knew that before he married you. (Field notes)

STRATEGIES FOR SECRECY. Only a minority of gay people share their secret with straights, and only a few chosen straights at that. But gay people in our society inhabit multiple worlds, only one of which is gay; since the rest are straight, the gay must use various strategies and tactics of concealment in his relationship with nongay people. Whereas a strategy is an overall plan of action with reference to secrecy, tactics are the actions taken in given settings to further concealment. For gays, a major strategy is the construction of a straight *front* for use in the straight world, and the main tactics involve the upkeep of that front and its adaptation to circumstances.

* This is a not uncommon way of being forced out of the closet. Angry former wives or male lovers are a dependable source of information for family and friends.

A front, in Goffman's terminology (1959, pp. 22–24), is composed of appearance (dress, body language, hairstyle, and so on) and demeanor (attitude and verbalization toward the other actors in the setting). Although everyone is concerned with fronts and self-presentation, the homosexual passer's front must be particularly self-conscious and particularly careful:

> JOHN: I was always just scared to death that my family was going to find out, and I would go to any lengths not to have them. I think I am starting to adjust myself where—I've gotten the attitude now if it happens its going to happen, we're just going to have to sit down and discuss it and I'm not going to worry about it—I always used to, er, date the girls from the office, always trying to put up a pretense. I always made sure that my family, you know, knew who I was going out with. Now I don't particularly do it, er, and generally, er, it can be—so many people—you know, in—in this life will never refer to two men together to their parents—er—constantly, and I do now, I'm either, you know, talking about Roger and Sam, or Dean and Bob, or something like this, and if it's girls they're generally two girls' names involved, and I'm never speaking now, er, as, er, Mildred and Rex or something like that. (Tape-recorded interview)

Unlike "normal" people without a secret, John feels compelled to avoid stigmatization by strategy, specifically the presentation of a heterosexual front to his parents. As he says it, his past strategy was quite elaborate, complete with dates with girls, avoidance of naming one-sex couples, and so on. His present strategy is one of avoidance without hiding: avoiding the presentation of an elaborate straight front while not concealing possible cues to his secret identity. A final strategy, which John sees as a possible future outcome, is the dropping of the mask of neutrality and the revealing of his identity.

The observation of gay people in the tactical process of presenting straight fronts was among the most interesting of my research tasks. Quite a few times I was asked to accompany gay men to functions associated with work or family, which enabled me to observe the change in behavior and appearance:

> Danny asked me if I would go with him to his next company dance, and I said yes. I wondered what he would be like. He was quite camp in mannerism, and his voice had more of the characteristic gay tone (which cannot be reproduced on paper) than any of the other people that I knew at the time. He smoked cigarettes in a manner traditionally labeled "feminine," and often waited for other men to light it. His body language, too, was rather nelly*: he arched his back when he sat, and crossed his feet daintily, gesturing expansively with hands and wrists. He dressed in very soft, colorful fabrics with subdued but elegant style. When he picked me up that night he was the same as ever in his attitude toward me: what might be termed a polite male chauvinist. He always opened doors for me, guided me across the street with his elbow, was most solicitous, and pulled out my chair when we were in a restaurant—the traditional masculine role which most gay men liked to play with me and other women. When we arrived at the dinner, I remained aware of his behavior. I noticed that the attentions I took for granted were much greater than the other men had for their dates or wives, and that Danny did not eye the other women while ignoring me, look bored and distracted, or make comments about his colleagues' dates, as they did. His manner, however, was quite different than in the gay world: he held his cigarette "normally" and lit those of the other women.

* See Chapter 5, page 107.

> His voice was still soft, but was a little deeper and had
> lost the characteristic gay tones. He was dressed pretty
> much as usual. I saw a series of subtle changes, which
> amounted to an enormous total change in the
> presentation of self. Later, on the dance floor, I felt
> extremely strange and could not decide why. We were
> dancing to a slow tune, and Danny was a good dancer,
> but something was amiss. When I finally figured it out, I
> thought it was really funny but he didn't when I told
> him about it later: he had taken me into his arms in the
> traditional male manner, but with me in the lead
> position. (Field notes)

Tactically, then, the front that is presented may be uncon-
vincing, or lacking in necessary elements. The more the man
becomes accustomed to the gay world and its customs, the
less he will be accustomed to the straight world, and the
more his strategies and tactics may be ineffective. The
members are aware of this:

> Aaron took me to his annual company dinner-dance,
> which he had not attended for five years. He com-
> mented, "It's been so long since I took a girl out I had
> to sit down and try to think what you're supposed to
> do."(Conversation)

One danger is that the front may be constructed from a his-
torically past time period when the male was actually dating
girls, maybe actually heterosexual. In one case, where I accepted an invitation to a dinner dance, the man called me up
to ask what color my dress was so he could buy the correct
corsage. A second danger is that the front, as with any conscious deception, may be overplayed in an effort to com-
pensate for its lack of truth:

> Anselm and his crowd at first thought the party was
> gay, and came in kissing all the guys, which caused

some little old lady eyebrows to be raised quite high. I quietly mentioned to Anselm that the party was in fact mixed-straight, and the straights were not wise, which he would have noted had he not been so drunk. Anselm spread the word and his group immediately started paying heavy-handed attention to the women present, who didn't seem to quite know why all these strange men were demanding to dance with them, putting their arms around them, and drunkenly kissing them. Mario, a gay guy standing next to me, muttered, "Look at those overacting queens." (Field notes)

The dangers are not all strategic: some of the penalties of the secret bearing of stigma are emotional, especially where otherwise close relationships with straight people are concerned. For many members; the concealment of their identity from workmates or other nonintimate relationships has no emotional implications, but concealment from close relationships of family, friends, brothers, and children may indeed have a high cost of guilt, alienation, and eventually the attenuation of the relationship. To avoid emotional schizophrenia, avoidance may be the final course of action.

One strategy of secrecy is the construction of a heterosexual front; another is the schizophrenia of separating straight and gay people into separate settings as well as separate worlds. This is one of the basic strategies adopted by most secret gays, and it has important implications. Because of the separation itself, and because of the necessity for deception in the keeping of the secret, relationships and interaction with straight people become progressively attenuated over time. John, who was a homosexual for many years before he came out in the gay community, describes how his coming out led to the lessening of the more strenuous contacts with straights:

CAROL: Did you know any gay people before—

> JOHN: Very few. I seldom went out. I kept my friends separated, literally, between a straight and a gay life . . . at the present time I no longer work for the company I used to, and my association now with people is almost literally—with the gay set of people, and as far as straight people are concerned, I see some of my friends periodically, and I call them, but—er—I very seldom ever have any social obligations with them.
>
> CAROL: Do you prefer this?
>
> JOHN: Yes. It's much more comfortable for me now. . . .
>
> (Tape-recorded interview)

Again, the stigmatization which underlies the construction of fronts implies the attenuation of the straight world and the enlargement of the gay world in importance and meaning for the gay individual.

As identity is established within the gay community, and social relationships and sociability with other members increase, there tends to be a corresponding decrease in interaction with the straight world. Not wishing to make the effort to attend the company dinner, the insurance agent goes to a gay party instead—he now has an alternative. Tired of inventing girl friends to satisfy the curiosity of his mother and father, the middle-aged man goes to live in another town, or picks a quarrel with his family and refuses to see them again. As gay identity and community relationships expand, straight relationships (always practically difficult and emotionally draining) contract.

In the irony which was recognized by the labeling theorists, the development of a secret gay world through stigmatization produces an amplification and intensification of the experience of being gay; it is no accident that overt gay groups are often less exclusive in their interaction and identity than secret groups (see Humphreys, 1971, 1972). The secrecy of gay identity in significant relationships, as well as in interaction, makes it both more poignant and more important for the self; the isolation of the gay community makes it more of a haven. The ultimate strategy of secrecy is withdrawal.

# 5. GAY KNOWLEDGE

A viable social world must be distinguished linguistically from other worlds. In the absence of any distinction between straight and gay, say in a society where bisexuality is the rule, there would be no gay world. The linguistic designation of a world, moreover, has several levels. The simplest level is a special vocabulary used by the members of the world. The most complex is the symbolic universe (an elaborate symbolic representation of the world in metaphysical, mythical, or religious terms; see Berger and Luckmann, 1967, pp. 92-128). An intermediate level includes *ideology*, which provides political justifications for the existence and positive values of the world, and *mythology*, which legitimates the world through legends, anecdotes, morality tales, and other symbolic representations.*

* Berger and Luckmann use the terms vocabulary, rudimentary or incipient legitimation, theoretical legitimation, and symbolic universe in order of complexity (1967, pp. 92-128).

GAY VOCABULARY. Gay and straight are the most significant words in the gay vocabulary. They dichotomize the world of the homosexual into "them" and "us," and by doing so provide a place for the self in the world of "us." As elaborated in Chapter 7, although the term "straight" means both sexually and culturally heterosexual, the term "gay" has a cultural as well as a sexual element that the term "homosexual" does not.

Straight and gay dichotomize identity, as well as sexuality and lifestyle. The term "gay" is used with the verb "to be"— a person is designated as *transsituationally being* gay, as a substantial self, rather than just *situationally being* a pedestrian, say, or *doing* a given activity (playing golf.) Within the gay world, other words index meanings particular to that world and set off *different types* of gay identity, gay community, and gay self.


*Identity Words.* Identity words used within the community (nouns and adjectives) are those that, within the general identity gay, describe specific subtypes of gay identity. For example, the wearing of female clothing (on the face of it a unitary act) may be interpreted in different ways according to the verbal designations transvestism, transsexualism, drag, or radical drag.

*Transsexualism* is a word used both within the gay world and within the straight world, to designate a person who wears female clothes and identifies with the female gender. In its scientific meaning, transsexual refers to a person who has undergone sex-gender transformation through surgery and supports this change by hormone treatments, cosmetics, clothes, roleplaying, and self-image. There is a small community of self-designated transsexuals in Sun City who do not, however, fulfill these scientific criteria in full but who still define themselves that way. Three of them, for instance, dressed and identified as women and took hormone shots, but they had not undergone sex-transformational surgery and wore their skirts so short that their male genitals were clearly visible through their female underwear.

Straight scientists, and many other gay and straight persons, would refer to these self-labeled transsexuals as *transvestites*. Again, in its scientific formulation, a transvestite is a person (usually a male) who may be heterosexual or homosexual in choice of sex object, but who habitually wears the clothes of the opposite sex, often with a masturbatory purpose. Unlike transsexuals, transvestites have the gender identity of their own sex and do not wish to undergo surgery to change. Neither transsexualism nor transvestism is an acceptable identity within the gay community, despite the fact that some members of the community, on occasion, dress as women.*

The term *drag* is used in the gay world to describe a person who wears female clothes and avoids the unacceptable imputations of transvestism or transsexualism. Drag is worn in the spirit of camp, and it is the most extreme expression of camp; camp, in turn, is lighthearted, spoofing behavior appropriate to the sociability settings of the gay community:

> CAROL: Could you—um—you mentioned high camp behavior and camp behavior. Could you describe some of this for us?
> SEBASTIAN. Oh. Yeah.
> CAROL: OK.
> SEBASTIAN: Very definitely. I think its mainly the idea of not necessarily wanting to be feminine—I have no desire to be a woman in any way, shape or form. But

* Transsexuals and transvestites may also disapprove of homosexuals.

again, gay kids are characterized. . . if you're female, for instance, the girls are often pictured as very masculine, very robust, and very butch. And the gay guys are pictured as being rather nelly,† you know, rather feminine, so—mainly I think endearing type terms like Stella, Mary. . . .

CAROL: Camp names.

SEBASTIAN:. . . and Grace, yeah, camp names. Yes, camp names that say, you know, I'm calling you Grace, you know, and who cares, you know, its a name so like very many other names—it could very easily be your name as a matter of fact, but, er, so far as dancing and drag, I think drag is probably something very foreign to most people in the straight realm, and its really nothing more than—than fun, than acting, as I said again, you have—you have certain people that get carried away with—er—the idea of drag, and they become transvestites, but—talking about these people is quite foreign to me, because I neither socialize nor know people like that. They're completely in another dimension, you might say, for me, so I have no idea of knowing exactly how they feel or why they feel the way they do.

CAROL: The thing that you last said that interested me was the difference between what you're saying is this transvestite, and drag. And I wondered—I can see what you mean, but could you explain it more?

SEBASTIAN: Yes, of course, I think—um—well, I don't think I really know, when it comes to drag—um—the main difference is—drag to most gay kids is sort of—is a fun thing—I mean, being more feminine, possibly, as most of the gay guys are—it's really sort of a camp, you know, sort of a parody, a play on things. There are a lot of gay kids in drag that have the idea that maybe they have prettier legs than most women, that they are more elegant than most women, you know, well this is a fixa-

† See page 107.

tion, I think that's really—not to be, you know, taught us—or—not something that's going to cause a lot of trouble, let's put it that way. Its merely something that they do in fun, where, you get into transvestites, and as I say, physically, I know, the hormone shots to stop the growth of hair, you know, to activate the mammary glands, and then they go into silicone bust shots and things like this—now, well to me this—a person very definitely has a problem all of their own—again, its not for me to say that its bad, that its good, because I remain very indifferent about the whole thing. (Tape-recorded interview)

CAROL: You mentioned earlier that you had to switch vocabularies when straight people are around. What did you mean?
JOHN: Well, there's a lot of expressions that you use— er, camp names. I'm not in favor of it, but God alone knows I get one hung on me, and I get thrown on—
CAROL: Tell me what it is!
JOHN: I get it thrown around here in the household when I walk into a bar—well, for some reason, and this was many, many years ago, and it came through a straight person, and it was just done accidentally, someone called me "Fluff." And it has stuck with me ever since, and I walk into a bar now and everyone hollers out "Fluffy." Generally they refer to people as either Josephine, or Agnes, or Cynthia, or what the hell ever the case may be. Why I don't know, but they hang these—these feminine names on them. And you have a tendency to get carried away with it once in a while, regardless of how masculine you're trying to be in a general sense of life . . . no matter what level of the so-ciety you are on, everyone does it—they just kind of camp and carry on. (Tape-recorded interview)

Camp behavior, camping and carrying on, female name and pronoun use, all describe behavior which is unserious, fun, episodic, and a parody of femininity, without implying female gender or deviance for the participants. These types of behavior include exaggerated gestures of the hand and body, a lisping speech style, and, at the highest camp—drag, the caricaturing of female clothing, behavior, and role.

The key terms in this description are caricature, fun, unserious, and episodic. Whereas transvestism or transsexualism sometimes represent a serious attempt to mimic femaleness, drag is always a parody and an exaggeration of all the things that imply theatrical or pin-up femininity in our society: long ballgowns and gloves, towering and elaborate coiffures, glittering jewerly, colorful and heavy makeup, a deep cleavage, or lots of leg showing. That drag is not simply a mimicry of women is indicated by the fact that women can get into drag too:

> Christophers is crowded Halloween night and a few of the regulars are in drag. I go to the ladies room, puzzled why the bartender has tried to stop me. I get quite a surprise—to the level of shock. There is Annie, the straight woman owner of the bar, getting into drag—substituting her own short plain brown hair for an elaborate blonde wig and her usual knit dress and stubby shoes for a glittering gown, long sleeves, and spike heels. A drag queen is in the ladies room helping her put on this drag, and showing her how to apply a long pair of fake eyelashes. Annie warns me "not to tell anyone," and I return to the bar! About five minutes later Annie and her companion make a grand entrance—two drag queens. For a moment nobody recognizes her, then they do. She is playing the drag queen to the hilt, her usual walk has been replaced by a swaying burlesque movement, and her hands and face faithfully mimic the drag queen gestures which she has probably learned from years of observation. (Field notes)

Drag is unserious and fun, or it becomes a way of life, and therefore an identity. Whereas transsexuals and transvestites wear female clothes because their very self-image depends on it, gay people get into drag to celebrate the ritual occasions of the gay world, like Halloween. A drag queen, who is somewhere between the transvestite and the man who gets into drag once in a while, wears drag fairly often but still only on appropriate occasions: for example, if the person is a female impersonator in a show.

In a similar way, the adjective "nelly" describes a kind of behavior and demeanor somewhere between the ritualized and limited fun of camp and the deviance of transvestism or extreme effeminacy. A nelly person, or nelly queen, is one who is not quite beyond the pale of community acceptability, but who is often a little too effeminate and flamboyant for safe secrecy about gayness:

> DONOVAN: Marlo is a nelly queen really, but she's OK, she can shape up when she wants to, and you can take her most places. I wouldn't want my boss to see us walking down the street though! (Conversation)

As this conversation shows, nelly queens, drag queens, and other community types are often referred to by the female pronouns "her" and "she" as well as given female names. Almost anyone in the gay community is subject to this kind of naming, either all or most of the time, or just when the member is acting camp; the names are generally linked with the man's given name, like Erica for Eric, Josephine for Joe, and Alice for Allan:

> I was quite surprised when after an evening's drinking and mirth Beckett referred to the dignified Horace as Hilda, but I noticed that Horace was camping and carrying on in a manner most unusual for him. Usually, he was a most reserved, quiet and traditional-masculine type. (Field notes)

More flamboyant than a nelly queen, because he is lots louder and less amenable to the preservation of secrecy, is a screaming queen. In a way, screaming queens (or screamers) are the opposite of the ideal-type transsexual, who seeks only to settle down quietly and anonymously into the world of women. Although transsexuals can be indistinguishable from women, screamers are flamboyant, flaunting both their gayness and their male effeminacy, and generally unconcerned about guarding their own secrecy or that of others:

> OLIVER: I'm always afraid one of those screaming queens I know from the bars will come rushing at me shrieking when I'm walking by my school. Those types of people don't have any sense.* (Conversation)

Radical drag, which involves the same act of wearing female clothing, again has a different meaning for identity within the gay world. Laud Humphreys says of radical drag:

> Radical drag differs from traditional transvestism ... in that there is no attempt to present a consistent and deceptive performance of the opposite sex role. (1972, p. 164)

> Radical drag is more than a technique, it is a new style of revolution that penetrates to the genitals of the system it calls to account. (1972, p. 170)

Radical drag, typified by the wearing of evening dress and gloves with boots and a beard, has political implications the other words do not have. I am required to use the work of Humphreys to clarify radical drag, because the community I studied within the gay world is largely apolitical and uses drag in one or another context of secrecy: in gay settings or

---

* For just this reason, Oliver and many other professionally occupied members of the gay community prefer to live quite a distance from where they work.

as a complete disguise within the straight world. Radical drag is designed as a political strategy to freak out the straight world overtly.

Radical drag is an aspect of a gay community that in many ways is alien and antithetical to the sociability community described here. Although radical drag has an element of comedy, it also has a deadly serious intent: a proclamation of revolution against the fact that certain worlds have power over other worlds, in this case the gay over the straight. Although some gay liberation activists affiliate with other movements, like the Chicano, black, or poor movements, the majority are what Humphreys calls "one-issue" organizations (1972, pp. 121–134).

In general, the gay liberation movement is opposite to the type of community described here. Whereas the gay liberationists are overt in their taking of a gay identity, the gay community is covert and secret. Whereas the life rounds of secret gays are segregated in time, place, interaction, and relationships by the terms gay and straight, gay activists attempt to inject their gay identity into all phases of their life rounds. And whereas the activists are politically radical and in sympathy with oppressed groups, the secret community tends to be either apolitical or fairly conservative. In Humphreys' terminology, secret gays are stigma evadors; the gay liberationists confront and transform their stigma (1972, pp. 134–149).

*Community Words.* Some words describe relationships and interactions within the chosen gay community. Interestingly, several words used to describe community relationships are social kinship words like mother, auntie, and sister, indicating the intimate and yet superficial character of those relationships (as opposed to the intimate and deep nature of bonds of friendship or marriage). Gay people are bound by bloodlike ties of fate and community as are aunts and nephews or mothers and sisters, and their sociable interaction has the same formal and obligatory character as visits from relatives.

The term "mother", for example, describes a person within the community with whom the members can have a special type of relationship, similar to an intimate yet superficial relationship with a middle-class mother in our society. The mother in the gay community is an older man past the prime of sexual life, who is both extremely camp and highly sociable. In the elite gay community the mother is generally just sociable; in the career community he may be more outrageous and effeminate, or even a drag queen. The mother's function is twofold: to engage intensively in sociability and contribute amusement to sociable events and to assist other people with advice and sympathy on various aspects of gay life, from drag to relationships with the family of origin, or sexual liaisons. The mother, if he is flamboyant enough, can also be called an "old queen" which sometimes has a negative tone.

Those members of the gay world (generally career gays) who attend drag balls and enter drag contests elevate their mothers to the status of "dowager queen" or "dowager empress," giving them a role supportive to the new, young, drag queens. "Princesses," "empresses," and other honorific titles are given to the contest winners. Each geographical area of cities on the West Coast of the United States, like Los Angeles and San Francisco, has a gay "royal family" whose "court" reigns for a year by election and then is replaced by another court at the annual drag ball for each area. Sun City has no official royal family, but there are persons in the bar network who take on semiformally the roles of empress, duchess, and so on.

Like the term "mother," the term "auntie" is generally used to designate a person rather than in direct address. An auntie, or old auntie, is, like a mother, an aging, somewhat effeminate, and socially powerful homosexual who attracts a circle of young men to whom he gives advice and sometimes money and shelter. Like mothers and old queens, aunties are often the wealthier members of the gay community, substituting, with age, the status criterion of money for that of good looks:

> JASON: I can't stand that old auntie. I feel sorry for him, all that money and all those young guys hanging around him waiting till he dies. You see him everywhere, too. (Conversation)

To a lesser extent, members of the secret gay community refer to co-members of about the same age as "sisters." This indicates a formalized, close, yet superficial relationship with the most important members of the cliques to which one belongs. In the radical-activist gay community, the same term may refer either to fellow male gays, to liberationist women in general, or to gay women in particular.

The word "lover" is the most frequently used in the description of the long-term sexual relationship, although the members sometimes (and sometimes humorously) use "husband" or "wife." As expanded in Chapter 4, the relational expectation implied by "lover" is similar in most respects to the dyadic intimate, sexual relationship of marriage in conventional society with its attendant emotional commitment, but often without the prescription of sexual fidelity, and sometimes without living together in the same household.*

Other sexual relationship terms describe the objective and short-term nature of many sexual contacts within the gay community. The term "trade," for example, refers to a man who is willing to be fellated by another man, but will not

---

* This separation is sometimes chosen, but often a result of job-linked moves to other geographical locales.

fellate his partner in turn. A "size queen" is someone very interested and even preoccupied with penis size, whereas a "shrimp queen" refers to a preoccupation with another area of the anatomy: toes. These descriptive nouns, which typify and sort people quite clinically with respect to their sexual preferences in casual contacts, could be extended to cover every conceivable variety of sexual behavior. Corresponding, of course, are argot words that describe the acts themselves: "blowing " for oral intercourse, "browning" for anal intercourse, and "golden shower" for urination with sexual implications.

Clearly, the words used in support of community and sexual relationships reflect the nature of the types of interaction expected. A short-term sexual relationship is supposed to be objective and similar to the *gesellschaft* relationships between a producer and a consumer; the long-term sexual relationship and the community relationship itself are *gemeinschaft*: close, primary and familial in nature, although with different degrees of superficiality and intimacy. As Simmel comments, such relationships result from the secrecy of the group and transcend other potentially primary affiliations such as the family of origin and the work relationship (1950, p. 369).


*Outsiders and Insiders.*    Gay and straight, dichotomizing ones world, community, and identity, have an absolute nature. But, as always, reality tends to be more complex than ideal types, and there are many ambiguities of persons, places, and roles that are potentially threatening to the dichotomization of gayness and straightness, which point to the need for finer differentiation of insiders and outsiders. Within the gay world, then, are terminologies that help to reduce ambiguities by defining and categorizing them.

The most obvious ambiguity is bisexuality as it is conventionally defined: sexual attraction and/or relationships with members of both sexes. In this case, the gay world shares some terminology with straight worlds such as swingers. Bisexuals are variously referred to as "bi," "AC/DC" or "switch-hitters."

Sexuality, however, is not the only arena of ambiguity. There are sometimes persons present within gay sociable interaction (besides the now-ubiquitous researchers) who cannot be designated either as "gay" (a full community member or "straight" (a complete outsider). These persons are usually heterosexual females and very infrequently are heterosexual couples. Such straight participants in gay community life are referred to as "wise," meaning that although they are heterosexual they interact sociably with the gay community and have positive feelings toward gay people (see also Goffman, 1963, pp. 28–31).

Heterosexual females are singled out for a special tag: "fag hag," on the West Coast; "fruit fly" or "faggotina" elsewhere. A fag hag is a name used among members, but not to the face of the woman so described, to refer to a heterosexual woman who socializes (sometimes exclusively) in the gay community. Such women are common in some cliques and rare or unknown in others; in either case, they tend to be single or divorced, often middle aged, and at least theoretically uninterested in sexual contacts with the gay males.

A final type of outsider, not quite an outsider but also not an insider, is the "closet queen,"* The appellation "queen" indicates that this type of man is partly included in the gay world since he is homosexual; "closet" modifies membership by a double secrecy. Although the community is a secret one,

* The overt gay community refers to such secret gays as "closet queens" because the secret gays maintain a double secrecy.

homosexuals are not supposed to be secretive with each other; thus the use of the term closet queen both is derogatory and implies an outsider. Vividly, it depicts the double secret homosexual as a lurker in closets, just as fag hag gives a clear picture of what such a woman might be like.

The important point is that everyone (and every kind of sexuality) be accounted for by some linguistic category of the gay world. Words, then, function to separate outsiders from insiders, to account for ambiguous persons within sociable or sexual interaction, and to describe the primary, close, and unique relationships of insiders with one another. In such a way is a world set apart from other worlds, emptionally as well as cognitively.

GAY LEGENDS AND LITERATURE. Gay legends, aphorisms, myths, and cautionary tales appear in conversation and in gay literature. In addition to gay literature, gay people are consumers of straight books and movies with gay themes or implication. The distinction rests on the nature of the intended audience: straight literature is intended for mass consumption, whereas gay literature is directed at the gay world. Both this distinction and the characteristic quality of gay books can be seen by the following book review extracts from a gay magazine:

> *Flight Sixty Nine* by Teryl Andrews. Have you ever wondered what it would be like to travel on an airline which catered to your kind of people, with sexy stewards instead of leggy stewardesses? . . . Our hero pilot is Douglas Cord (as in Rip). Of course he has a guy in every port. He's young, hung, and handsome, natch. Oh yea, there's even a plot, although you need not let that detain you, it doesn't block the action. (*California Scene*, 1970, p. 12)

> *Blue Movie* by Terry Southern. . . . author Southern uses two thinly disguised film beauties (females, that is) performing a sixty-nine in glorious color for art's sake as one of the many mad episodes in this latest novel from World Publishing ($6.95). I found the lesbian sequences (and curiously the homosexual encounters are usually lesbian in straight novels and films—someone's obviously afraid of the big bad wolf) sexy and fascinating: they are probably among the most erotic lesbian sequences ever written. (*California Scene*, 1970, pp. 13–15)

Members of the secret gay community may read gay novels from time to time, but they are avid consumers of straight novels and films with gay themes, and they are highly critical of them. The movies "Boys in the Band" and "Staircase," for example, were critized by most members who saw them as too negative and as insensitive and stigmatizing depictions of the gay scene. "The Fox," however, was much acclaimed by gay males (although not by lesbians) as typical of a lesbian relationship.

Aside from media communications, which are basically fictional, both conversation and literature  purvey gay legends or myths based on "known fact"—most particularly legends of famous people who are supposed to be gay. These people range from contemporary (and quite obvious) movie stars who are given tags like "Mr. Visually Virile," to most of the significant historical figures of the past and present. And if they are not gay, they are bisexual:

> Turning to the one towering figure in all English drama, William Shakespeare, one can say the contribution is overwhelming. But did Shakespeare's alleged homosexuality influence his writing in any way? . . .
> And what of Christopher Marlowe? This mercurial figure, dead at the age of 29 in a tavern brawl, was ru-

moured to have liked boys. Indeed it has been surmised
that the brawl was precipitated by a slighting reference
to his current lover. . . .

   Critics of Edward Albee have hammered away at the
idea that he purposely shields his true intent by making
his characters heterosexual, and point to *Who's Afraid
of Virginia Woolf?* Saying it's really about two gay couples and not the way its presented at all. (Starr, 1971,
p. 10)

These kinds of gay myth appear not only in gay publications
but in sociological ones as well, along with legends of special
gay creativity and sensitivity (see Humphreys, 1972; Schofield, 1965).

GAY IDEOLOGY.   Gay ideology, like gay vocabulary, is dif-
ferentiated by the political activism or covert secrecy of the
particular gay community. Gay ideology makes explicitly legitimating statements about gay identity, community, and
way of life, either politically or less so.

   Less political ideology statements, found conversationally
and in conservative as well as radical gay publications, are
representations of the gay life as superior in various ways to
the straight life, and sometimes of the straight life as cor-
respondingly inferior. Donald Webster Cory, a gay psychiatrist, has some typical statements on the superiority of gay in
several areas:

   The high levels of intelligence frequently encountered
   among homosexuals have been readily conceded.
   (1951, p. 148)

   A true and genuine democracy so frequently pervades
   the activities of the homosexual group . . . the
   deeprooted prejudices that restrict marriages and

friendships according to social strata . . . are conspicuously absent among . . . the homosexual society. (1951,
p. 152)

[The homosexual] is forced to obtain a wealth of
knowledge about the personal psychological makeup of
individuals, he can and frequently does apply this to a
fuller understanding of others. And when to this understanding is added compassion for all individuals and
groups . . . a rare combination of worthwhile traits is ob-
tained. (1951, pp. 153–154).

Again, sociological "experts" often concur in these types of
judgment (see above; also see Humphreys, 1972, pp.
63–77). Gay legitimators jump at statements by straight
experts that ideologically legitimate gay life; (witness the
frequent quotes by lesbians of Kinsey's postwar statement
that straight men should learn from gay women how to make
love to woman):

The United States is eventually going to have to make a
complete turnaround on sex laws, from repressing to
encouraging nonreproductive behavior, sex researcher
Paul Gebhard says. (*The Advocate*, 1971, p. 11)

The highly political legitimation of gayness is more complex, since the political groups concerned with the issue form
a spectrum from the conservative Mattachine Society and
Society for Individual Rights to the radical Gay Liberation
Front (GLF) and Gay Activists Alliance (GAA), closely
paralleled by a similar spectrum of gay literature (newspapers, journals, and magazines). The conservative organizations, like the conservative ethnic group organizations such as
the NAACP, campaign for gay legal and social rights in a
traditional reformist manner. The GLF and GAA have much in
common with other activists in our society like the Black

Panthers; they rely on demonstrations, martyrdom tactics, and occasional violence (see Humphreys, 1971, 1972). Thus although one conservative journal applauds consumer boycotts of businesses hostile to gays, the editors also express their distaste for radical activism:

> The time has come for homosexuals to prove that they also have a buying power to be reckoned with. The studios have shown no reluctance about using homosexuality in movies to make money . . . they try to make a buck from gay audiences on the one hand, and have their spokesmen making derogatory slurs on this same audience on the other. (*California Scene*, 1970, p. 31)

> The dinner for Assemblyman Willie Brown, Jr., (given by a homophile group) was a success . . . the Gay Liberation folk, present, some of whom wore only trousers, kept jumping up and down . . . finally, to the delight of everyone else present, he told them off in no uncertain terms.(*California Scene*, 1970, p. 3)

THE SYMBOLIC UNIVERSE. A symbolic universe integrates a given world of meaning into a whole system, often using the symbols of religion or metaphysics to do this. Within the symbolic universe, the member learns the history of the group, is socialized and in turn socializes new members, and sets his biography in a new context. The symbolic universe is the ultimate legitimation of both identity and world, since it integrates the two within the sweep of history and the future.

United States society is a symbolic universe. A person is born "an American" and learns to differentiate himself or herself from other peoples, learning also the "superiority" of Americanism. The world of Americanism is supported by various symbols, such as the flag and the national anthem, that link the present with history and with supernatural forces. More mundane symbolisms, like "mom and apple pie" link everyday existence with the symbolic universe.

Gay persons in our society are born into this symbolic universe, and for many of them the American-Puritan tradition has been a crucial element in their socialization and identity formation. The transition to a gay community, identity, and world thus necessitates a partial change of the symbolic universe. The change remains partial because, through socialization, geography, and—in the case of the secret gay community—acceptance, gay people remain within the symbolic universe of the United States as a whole, but at the same time they move to another world with its own (potentially alienative) symbolic universe.

That part of the gay world that most significantly challenges the social symbolic universe is gay sexuality, which is anathema to traditional gender identity and sexual orientation in the Puritan sexual code. Because of this, the sexuality of a gay person retains the clearest potential for alienation from the American symbolic universe (see Humphreys, 1972), and remains the most carefully preserved core of the gay world itself. Violations of the norms of sociability call for only playful sanctions, whereas violations of homosexuality by bisexuality or heterosexuality can lead to exclusion from the group (see Chapter 6) or to the application of what Berger and Luckmann call therapy—diagnosis and cure of deviance (which of course is just what straight society does to gays, who challenge basic sex and gender roles, not just etiquette):

> OLIVER (discussing Bill's marriage): It will never work—once gay always gay—he'll be back in the group. I give him a year. I guess he did it for his family. (Conversation)

In nonsexual matters, there are various attempts at integration between the gay world and the American symbolic universe, as well as actions designed to foster alienation and separation. At the political level, this takes the form of the fundamental human right under the Constitution for full socioeconomic participation of gays in the society, counterpointed by a demand to change that system itself by gay revolution. There are two other levels of possible integration or separation, the religious and the mundane.

Gay religious organizations are generally integrative; they have as their main concern the acceptance of gays within the various churches and denominations, in integrated or separate congregations, of American society (the Metropolitan Community Church is one such offshoot). The publications of gay religious bodies are interesting; they illustrate the simultaneous use of the themes of Christian brotherhood and community in the Christian symbolic universe, and of the separate interests of the gay community. Articles on gay festivals and new bars coexist with traditional Christian rhetoric:

> Who am I? I am a servant of God. My Life is ruled through and by Him and my faith continuously inspired by him. My thoughts, His thoughts, my actions, His actions. . . . Because of these beliefs, I feel God has led me to organize and begin [the New Church of Christ] as a church of the living god. (*Exodus*, 1970, p. 10)

> Sun City's newest Sin Spot . . . has opened. Opening night saw many of the Metropolitan Community Church girls there besides this reporter . . . there were Bill, Dick, Bob, Matt, both Ken's (sic) (who had a difficult time dancing together) and too many others. (*The Prodigal*, 1971, p. 5)

At the mundane level, gay people and straight people bridge gaps in simple interactional ways, gradually eroding the perception of many straights that persons labeled "deviant" tend to have two horns and a tail:

> I showed my Social Problems class a publication of the Metropolitan Community Church. One student, amazed, said, "You mean that homosexuals actually go to church like normal people?" (Field notes)

A naive straight person perusing the pages of a gay journal might be surprised, too, to find all kinds of typical articles: meatless recipes, cookbook ads, astrology—all with a gay content, but quite mundane in form.

KNOWLEDGE, STIGMA, AND SECRECY. At levels of legitimation from vocabulary to the symbolic universe, the body of gay knowledge sampled here both differentiates the gay world from the straight and provides links between the worlds. In this sense, Simmel's observation that "the secret society lives in an area to which the norms of the environment do not extend" must be challenged (1950, p. 360). Although the "norms of society" are modified in some parts of the gay experience (such as sexuality and the quality of relationships), there are other areas in which gayness is not distinct from straightness, at least within the secret community (like astrology and sociability norms). Thus gay knowledge has two tasks: to teach the differentness of gay as well as its sameness.

Clearly, the amount and kind of differentness and sameness vary with the gay community. Gay activist groups, for example, often stress the need to isolate the gay political stance from that of other oppressed peoples, whereas other gay activists seek cooperation with ethnic minorities, the poor, and women. In this particular secret community, the sameness extended to the worlds of work, the family of origin, and the political, socioeconomic, and religious arenas; whereas the differentness was confined to gay community interactions and relations and the establishment of a hidden gay identity.

In any other contest, most of the men and women in the community were, to me, indistinguishable from straight people, conforming to general norms of demeanor, dress, appearance, voice, and conversation. In the gay context, however, almost all were transformed to one extent or another. The word gay, whose origins are etymologically unclear, is descriptive of the kind of liveliness experienced by the members in this transition (which Berger calls ecstasy): the dropping of the mask, the putting on of the true identity, the ritual celebration of brotherhood enhanced by stigma and secrecy, and the sexuality experienced within this world of meanings. The secrecy and the stigma themselves add an inestimable poignancy to the experience;

> Through the symbolism of the ritual, which excites a whole range of vaguely delimited feelings beyond all particular, rational interests, the secret society synthesizes those interests into a total claim upon the individual. By means of the ritual form, the particular purpose of the secret society is enlarged to the point of being a closed unit, a whole both sociological and subjective. (Simmel, 1950, p. 360)

II. SOCIETY

# 6. SOCIETY AND STIGMA

In taking on a gay identity and living within the gay world, a person takes on a stigmatized identity and lives within a world rendered secret by that stigmatization. In making such a commitment, he reverses much of what he has learned growing up in American society and takes a most fateful stance toward the future.

Today, and perhaps even more so when today's gay people were growing up, homosexuality in most people's eyes is not a good lifestyle to choose. If not sin, it has connotations of sickness; even for the most liberal groups in our society (the academics, perhaps?), homosexuality retains a taint of strangeness and unwholesomeness. There are very few straights who take gay for granted in a natural way. Joseph Epstein's recent diatribe against homosexuality caused a stir in both the gay and the intellectual worlds, but it seems typical:

> In the beginning, I felt confusion, revulsion, and fear. I must have been nine or ten years old when my father . . . who carefully instructed me never to say the word "nigger," one night sat me down in our living room to explain that there were "perverts" in the world. These were men with strange appetites, men whose minds were twisted, and I must be on the lookout for them . . . . There were not many such men in the world, but there were some, and they might wish to "play" with my brother and me in ways that were unnatural. (1970, p. 37)

A person who identifies himself as homosexual or gay, even tentatively, can either accept stigmatizing social definitions of himself as sick, sinful, or weird, or he can neutralize them and come to regard his new self as positive and good. Given the first choice, many homosexuals go to psychiatrists for cure, or to ministers for counsel; given the second, they go to the gay community, which has powerful ways of assisting in the neutralization of stigma. Some of the ways the gay world is legitimated as a separate, good, and beautiful world have already been discussed in the context of knowledge; the neutralization of stigma is the other side of this process. The ways in which this is accomplished are often those of the straight world; for their own purposes, gay people use straight theories of latency, deviance and normalcy, and mental illness and etiology, with as much conviction—but a different purpose—as straight stigmatizers.

LATENCY THEORY AND NIHILATION.     Nihilation, as used by Berger and Luckmann, is simply taking the sting out of stigma by implying that the stigmatizing audience is really the same at heart as the people they stigmatize:

> Therapy uses a conceptual machinery to keep everyone within the universe in question. Nihilation uses a similar machinery to liquidate conceptually everything *outside* the same universe. The threat of heterosexual life can be conceptually liquidated by looking upon it as inferior, no fun, sexually inhibited. Second, nihilation involves the more ambitious attempt to account for all deviant definitions of reality in terms of concepts belonging to one's own universe. For example, our homosexual theoreticians may argue that all men are by nature homosexual—or, at the very least, bisexual. Otherwise why are there such stringent laws against homosexuality? Antihomosexual prejudice can thus be transformed into secret desires—an affirmation of the homosexual universe which is ostensibly negated. (Berger and Luckmann, 1967, pp. 116–119)

The essence of latency theory as a device for nihilating the straight world is that all men are in some part homosexual. Even Epstein, the hostile intellectual, is willing to consider such a possibility:

> If I had the power to do so, I would wish homosexuality off the face of the earth—I find myself completely unable to come to terms with it.
> Why can't I come to terms with it? Is it the fear of the latent homosexuality in myself, such as is supposed to reside in every man, which makes this impossible? (1970, p. 51)

There are two versions of a latency theory of homosexuality within the gay world: the theory that all men are latent homosexuals in the sense of Freud's theory of primal bisexuality and repression, and the theory that all men are "to be had" (TBH). Freudian theory is elaborated by the contention that the greater the adhorrence of homosexuality, the more that has had to be repressed—neutralizing society's stigmatization on a sort of sliding scale:

> SIMEON: Yeah, I think men are basically gay to some extent, all men. Just when they hate queers the most you know that they are more gay, and when they don't give a damn you know they're mostly straight. (Conversation)

Sometimes other persons (like parents) who taught the stigmatization of homosexuals are reinterpreted in this way.

> JEROME: My father used to talk about the fairies even when I was a kid—there were fairies at the bottom of his garden. Looking back, I realize he must have been gay, but couldn't let it out in the open, so, you know, it came out that he hated the fairies and talked about them all the time. (Conversation)

The TBH theory holds that all men are not latent homosexuals in their substantial selves, but are *situationally* liable to homosexual involvement. They are *latently sexually open* according to the situation:

> CAROL: Do you think that all men are basically gay?
> JUSTIN: No. But I think they're all TBH (laughs).
> CAROL: In what way?
> JUSTIN: Just that given the right time and place, and the right situation, any guy can be had. I ought to know. I've done it enough. But that doesn't mean that he's basically gay. He'll just go on and forget it. A guy that's basically gay, he'll do it but he'll be uptight and tell how he hates the queers. (Conversation)

These examples of nihilation are at a theoretical and explicit level; in addition, there is that implicit type of nihilation which occurs in everyday interaction, involving spoofing or satirizing the straight world. One way in which this is done is by interpreting, by implication, all straight phenomena as "really gay":

> A group of eight is watching the Academy Awards over cocktails and dinner; an institution among many cliques of the gay community. Whenever an actor comes on the screen, one of the gays makes a comment on the man's sexual history, genital endowments, or presentation of self, like "that one's a raving faggot," or "look at that queen, he must have had plastic surgery on that face," or "that one was Johann's lover, years ago." For the actresses are reserved comments like "where did that drag queen get that horrible outfit?" or "that dress is too much, she must have gotten it at the Goodwill."
>
> At the bullfight, watching one of the matadors, Oliver commented: "look at her flip that pink thing!" (Field notes)

This type of nihilation is characterized by the rendition of the straight world as impotent, laughable, harmless, and ultimately an aspect of the gay world. It is annihilated.

Another kind of satirizing nihilation is the definition of heterosexuality as a perversion of basic homosexual nature. This implication of the latency theories given above is made clear in the following excerpt from a spoof entitled "Everything You've Always Wanted to Know About Heterosexuality But Were Afraid to Ask":

> *What is male heterosexuality?* Heterosexuality is a dread disfunction (sic), malignant in character, which infects a surprising percentage of American males. . . .

> Through societal attitudes, pressures and conditioning,
> the infected individual infects others he comes in
> contact with. . . .
> *Why do some males cross the natural sex barriers to*
> *have sex with people of the opposite sex?* Most re-
> searchers believe that all individuals go through a
> heterosexual phase in early childhood. In post-pubertal
> heterosexuality, something goes wrong with the normal
> development pattern. The victims of this unfortunate
> condition attempt to escape from reality by crawling
> back into the security of the womb . . . . While
> regressing to this infantile behavior pattern, many
> heterosexuals suck on the breasts of the female as a
> preliminary. This infantile behavior is, of course, a
> reenactment of the breast feeding stage of infancy.
> *Can heterosexuality be cured?* . . .(Jackson, 1972, p. 9)

This satire also, of course, implicitly nihilates experts' "explanations" of homosexuality simply by turning their rhetoric
around and making fun of it. The total effect of this type of
multiple nihilation of the straight world, combined with legitimation of the gay world, is great, since it retains a familiar
and powerful rhetoric, while radically reshifting the cognitive
categories and values within that rhetoric—ultimately stigmatizing the stigmatizors. In this vein, the stigmatizors can be
perceived as inferior to the gays since, if they are latent, they
have by definition denied one aspect of their "basic selves": *

> TAYLOR: Gay people are just more honest than straight
> people—at some point in their lives they have admitted
> that they have that in them. (Conversation)

However it occurs, nihilation, as Berger and Luckmann
point out, is one of the most powerful stigma neutralizers a
world can use.

* Researchers report the same kind of stigma neutralization among prostitutes, who claim that they are the only moral and honest women, because they set a price for their services, whereas housewives don't.

DEVIANCE: MAINTAINING THE BOUNDARIES OF COM-
MUNITY.   As Durkheim (1960), Goffman (1963), and
Erikson (1966) noted, deviance is a vital component of any
society, because it highlights the boundaries of normalcy and
social expectations. The straight world is not the only one
that uses terms such as "deviant," "sick," and "pervert" to
describe people who are off limits; the gay world uses these
and similar terms in a parallel way. Among the gay world deviants in the community I studied were transsexuals, transvestites, pedophiles, and other "trash":

> SEBASTIAN: I wouldn't like trashy gay people. I think
> it's too bad that so much of the world judges all gay
> people and all gay kids, both girls and guys, by a few of
> the social deviants that, you know, throw a bad light on
> all of us. . . . [Some men] become transvestites—but—
> talking about these people is quite foreign to me, be-
> cause I neither socialize or know people like this.
> They're completely—in another—dimension, you might
> say, from me. (Tape-recorded interview)

In turn, and like gay people in straight society, the "deviants"
may object to stigmatization. In response to editorials in gay
journals critical of their sex practices, sadomasochists and
child lovers reply:

> Editor:
> . . . I object . . . to your use of the words "sadist" and
> "sadistic" in describing police behavior. . . . We have
> enough trouble as a result of the public's interpretation
> of sadomasochism, without our own brothers getting it
> wrong.
> A sadist is a lover, not a hater. Sadistic actions are
> acts of love, not hate.
> Whatever it may look like to someone who is not in
> the S & M* scene, the sadist is giving pleasure to his
> slave and derives pleasure from that fact . . . .

* Sadomasochists.

Lay off of us. We don't poison wells, throw rocks at children, kick dogs, or beat our mothers. We're good guys and deserve better than having the police compared with us. (*The Advocate*, 1971, p. 20)

Editor:
Regarding Jim Kepner's sympathetic (?) review of *A Crocodile of Choirboys*, I take exception to his placing pedophiles out in left field with the sadists . . . .
   I guess I'm just sick and tired of being equal with sadists, child killers, and other creeps. . . . Boy lovers, (most of us, I think, prefer that to pedophiles) simply love boys, and maybe in this screwed up world, that isn't such a bad quality. (*The Advocate*, 1971, p. 20)

By such mechanics of exclusion and inclusion, the gay community limits membership in the gay world to "normal queers." A normal queer is a negative typification. Normal queers are not drag queens or gay liberationists, do not engage in "bizarre" sexual practices, and do not flaunt their sexual preferences all over the straight world. However, "normal queers" do wear drag, camp around, and tease one another about whips and chains.

In general, the tolerated limit of *otherwise deviant* behavior within which the individual may act without exclusion from the group is marked by the concept of *fun* as discussed with reference to the contrast between transvestism, transsexualism, and drag. In a similar vein, camp behavior is within the tolerated limits of behavior as long as it is for fun, and not from the standpoint of "being that type of person" or "being effeminate" in a transsituational sense. Thus John, who says that "everyone" in the gay community acts camp from time to time, also stigmatizes those who typically engage in such behavior:

JOHN: (disdainfully): . . . screaming types . . . their actions are excessively exaggerated to the feminine stan-

dard—even a woman wouldn't act that way—they take
femininity and try to just overdo it. They high pitch their
voice, they scream at each other, and they call one
another Daisy, they probably never even knew what the
other person's name was. (Tape-recorded interview)

Even such otherwise stigmatized and intolerable deviances as
child molestation and sadomasochism are (verbally) tolerated
within the context of fun:

> RAINER: . . . and you know what I gave him for his
> birthday? A blonde wig and a whip. . . .
>
> SIMEON: Look at him look at that little kid!
> OLIVER: Oh, I like a bit of chicken* once in a while!

Transsexuals, pedophiles, and sadomasochists are
generally considered deviant within the straight as well as the
gay world, but the gay world excludes as deviant persons
who would be acceptable within straight society—married
men—and persons who would at least be less deviant than
homosexuals—bisexuals. As Cory comments, the gay community does not accept men married to women: "The submerged group life accepts with hesitance and deep re-
servation the married man. He is not one of them" (1953, p.
220).† Furthermore, those gay individuals who marry
women are presumed to be doing so for purposes other than
the general societal reasons of love, sexuality, and so on. The
interpretations again nihilate the straight world. Gay men
marry to please their families, because they are forced to, or
to punish recalcitrant male lovers:

> To each new arrival the news was announced: "Arno is
> getting married in San Francisco. Several people asked

---

* A sexually attractive young child.
† Cory, a gay psychiatrist, was married and experienced this exclusion.

"why?" The most popular explanation was that he was doing it to get back at his ex-lover Darian, who had left him for someone else. A second explanation was that he was doing it in order to put on a straight facade in his work. (Field notes)

If a person does marry, it is assumed that he will "inevitably" return to the gay world, since homosexuality is his basic nature. If he gets divorced, he will be welcomed back into the gay community; if he stays married, he will not be welcomed at all, except as a sexual partner:

CAROL: Have you met anyone who's been in this gay life and then left it and gotten married? Do you think that this is possible or . . . .

JOHN: Oh yes, a lot of men do—I assume that the women do too. Uh—I think in an awful lot of cases, from the ones that I do know, they got married, they have families, and they plan to stay out of it, but somewhere in the late years they kind of drift back. They may stay married and try to keep it away from their wives, but the majority of ones that I know that have been gay and gotten married after about five or six years, it seems like, of married life, they start going out every now and then.

CAROL: Why do you think this is?

JOHN: Well, I think, like anything it's very difficult to break the habit—you just don't particularly get away from it. You just drift back eventually into the relationship.

CAROL: Do you think it might be—they drift back into the sexual relationship or back into the friendship group?

JOHN: I think it's generally back into the sexual relationship, I think that's generally what it is. Because I don't know too many of the married guys that are on the social level of gay life . . . the ones that I do know and know socially are ones that have been gay—or—

not gay—have gotten married, and then dissolved their
marriage, and then gotten into the gay life or back into
it—and there's a lot of these—there's quite a few of
them.

CAROL: Do people who have children, and, say ex-
wives, do they talk about it much, or do you often get
surprised by them?

JOHN: I generally get surprised—er—they don't talk
about it as a general rule, the only time they talk about
it is with very close friends. (Tape-recorded interview)

Similarly, men who define themselves as bisexual are
generally excluded from the secret-sociable gay community,
although they may be welcome as bed partners. Bisexuality
as a self-definition is regarded both as an instance of bad
faith and as an exhibition of a lack of commitment to the gay
community. As the existentialists point out, bad faith is a self-
delusion, an escape from authenticity; most gay people regard those who designate themselves "bisexual" as copping
out from the polar choice gays see as the core of their lives.*
In their lack of commitment to the gay community, too,
bisexuals are seen as a threat to the preservation of secrecy;
as Simmel points out, secret and stigmatized communities
often require a deep loyalty and commitment from the
members as a means of preservation of the secret (1950, p.
348). Somewhat ironically, then, whereas sadomasochists
and other "deviants" are disliked for the same reasons that
straights stigmatize them,† the married and bisexuals are
disliked because of their affiliation with the straight world,
the stigmatizing audience.

* This may not be true of the overt gay communities. See Humphreys,
1971, 1972.

† In addition, many "normal queers" do not want their respectable fronts
tarnished by association with sadomasochists, child molesters, or deviants of other stripes. They are well aware that public differentiation of
these from homosexuals is unclear; the stereotype of "deviant" encompasses them, too.

MENTAL ILLNESS AND PARANOIA. "Mental illness" is one of the major rhetorics of our society and our times. Where once stigmatized persons were interpreted theologically as possessed by demons, or at the very least evil, today those same persons are dealt with by concepts of "sickness," with attendant theories of etiology, epidemiology, and cure. Homosexuals are often interpreted as "sick" by those who are unwilling to label them demonic; in turn, "normal queers" interpret those outside the boundaries of their community as sick:

> JEROME: You get into transvestites type thing—a person very definitely has a problem all of their own. . . . When you get into people physically wanting to change, it's a mental fixation, it's a type of feeling, I suppose where there's a feeling of inadequacy as far as being a man is concerned, or logically—um—a domineering mother, you know, a very weak father, a very unconcerned, possibly a strong father, but very unconcerned, so there are very many facets which—um—you could look at to say well this is the reason, that's the reason, and et cetera . . . .I don't think many gay kids really enjoy transvestites type thing. (Tape-recorded interview)

Normal queers, of course, do not agree to the stigmatizing society's definition of them as sick (just as transsexuals think that they are normal, but homosexuals are sick). There is, however, one psychiatric label to which gays willingly admit, but in a nonpsychiatric way: paranoia.

Secret gay people use the concept of paranoia to refer to their experience and reactions when confronted by the need to pass as a straight. As Lyman and Scott comment: "It is as a 'passer' that the homosexual exhibits the behavior sometimes called 'paranoid' by clinical investigators. The situations that are quite routine for normals become problematic for him" (1970, p. 78). Clearly, there is a distinction between this conception of paranoia (which is basically interactional) and that used by psychiatric experts (referring more to a condition of the self, stemming from past conditions):

> Homosexuals, who have sometimes been treated as clinically paranoid, can be seen as persons embedded in a permanently problematic environment so long as they inhabit heterosexually oriented societies. Their allegedly paranoid behavior—indicated by a heightened suspiciousness, conspiratorial interpretation of events, and strategies of deviance disavowal or concealment—can be seen as behavior oriented to their particular problematic status. (Lyman and Scott, 1970, p. 87)

SEBASTIAN: I don't withdraw, you know. I'm not paranoid about being around straight people. But I—I suppose I remain a bit more reserved when I'm around people that I know wouldn't or couldn't understand . . . people are . . . very aggressive, you know, they become completely paranoid, and people watching and looking—and, but again, a lot of kids—um—learn through experience, and gay kids are made to be paranoid because you always have to keep your left up, you know, you can't let down a minute, you know, you never can get too much to drink, that you might say something that you—you shouldn't say.
CAROL: You mean among straight people?
SEBASTIAN: Among straight people, yes. So you know you keep your defenses up constantly, um, which consequently makes most kids very cautious, very very paranoid to the fact that it starts bothering them, you know, they go someplace and they say, well, gee, I hope no one knows that I'm gay, you know, I hope that my facade of butchiness and straightness is coming across the—you know—loud and clear, yes, loud and clear, beep, beep, yes. (Tape-recorded interview)

Freud said that paranoid projection also plays a big role in homosexuality; in fact he eventually decided that ho-

mosexuality is a defense against paranoia . . . .In classic
paranoid fashion [the homosexual] projects onto
someone else the urge he cannot tolerate in himself.
(Karlen, 1971, pp. 265–266).

Clearly, the conceptions of paranoia used by Freud on the
one hand and by Lyman and Scott and the gay community
on the other are quite different. For Freud, paranoia is a
*cause* of homosexuality; continuing the medical model
analogy, homosexuality is a disease or sickness affecting the
entire personality. The members' conception, however, is that
paranoia is an interactional *effect* of homosexuality—more
specifically, secret homosexuality which the actor attempts to
conceal from stigmatizing straight audiences. In situations of
concealment, gays can easily exhibit a paranoid style.

ETIOLOGY, EPIDEMIOLOGY, AND CURE.    In the medical
model of deviance, the stigmatized are sick, and their
sickness—like any medical state—has a cause (etiology), an
incidence (epidemiology), and a cure. As a secret but committed community, gay people do not seek cure; they regard
it as undesirable, impossible, or both:

> ALVIN: I wouldn't change my life for anything. If
> someone asked me if I wanted to change, I would say
> no. I really like the gay life, and I am quite happy as I
> am.
> MITCHELL: Once gay, always gay. (Conversation)

Gay people within the secret community are, however,
concerned with both the incidence and cause of homosexuality. One difference between the secret community
and the overt community of gay liberationists is in the acceptance and use of etiological theories of homosexuality. The

following exchange between a student and a gay liberation speaker in a classroom situation illustrates the overt gays' attitude (see also Humphreys, 1972):

> STUDENT: What do you think causes homosexuality?
> LARRY: You might just as well ask what do you think causes heterosexuality?

This answer is reminiscent of recent sociological and psychoanalytic perspectives; however, the secret gay community, like more traditional sociologists and psychoanalysts, accepts a variety of etiological theories of homosexuality, but does not question the etiology of heterosexuality. Although some gays use biological rhetorics like "my hormones did it," the theory of "my family did it" is the major one, which, of course, is a causal rhetoric that has dominated the mass media and the educational system for several decades:

> JOHN: I think it's environment, and I would think it is—it's parents, and a lot has to do with yourself, but I still think it's basically the parents—I don't think it is a fault of theirs, you can't correct it because every time you see anybody or talk to anybody, they have an idea generally of why they went gay, if they have any common sense and want to sit down and try to analyze it, a lot of them probably don't, they just accept the fact that "I'm gay" and they probably don't every try to figure out why it may have happened—er—I would analyze my own situation in the fact that—er—I have a very dominant mother—in a lot of cases this is true, it isn't always true—a lot of men become very—just completely straight all through their lives and their mothers were dominant. There is something probably in their own character that—that—because of your mother being very dominant, and she was with—with my father—er—my first stepfather—it may have had a

chance of being different, because he was the dominant character, but unfortunately he was killed in the war—er—with my present stepfather, who is definitely the dominant character. Now I have a half-sister but she is also gay and I had never met my half-sister until about five or six years ago, because my mother divorced my original father when I was very young, and we moved to California. I was raised by my mother, my grandmother and my aunt, all very dominant women in their husbands' lives. My father unfortunately was the type that accepted this dominance, apparently, because when I went back East once, and I met my stepmother, my half-sister's mother, who is just like my mother, she is the dominant one, and my sister turned out gay—but I think in a lot of cases this determines it in a family. I think it's amazing how many brothers and how many sisters are gay, and you could attribute it, I think, to parental upbringing and the attitude of parents, because from what I know of my roommate and his brother who are both gay, the mother is again dominant, and you try to identify yourself somewhere along the line—so consequently your mother is dominant, and your father is being passive, in a man's case, and you're going to look for a dominant male somewhere along the line, you're going to try to find the dominant opposite person that you didn't have in your parents' lives. This is one of the questions if I was analyzing my own situation, this is why I would say that both my sister and I turned out gay.

CAROL: Do you think there is any changing once this is set?

JOHN: Do you mean could I change now? I don't believe so, as far as I'm concerned it's too late. I don't particularly care to change, because I'm very happy—I've adapted myself to it. (Tape-recorded interview)

There are several interesting aspects of this kind of theorizing. It indicates the possible "feedback effect" of etiological theories, in which psychological and other explanations of social phenomena are "fed back" by the members as "proof." Homosexuals who have learned, through the mass media and education, that homosexuals have dominant mothers, come to interpret their mothers as dominant (this may be especially true for homosexuals who seek psychiatric help). Also interesting is the "umbrella" use of popular rhetorics to cover all kinds of contingencies. Whereas, John used the rhetoric of dominant mothers to account for his own "normal queerness," Sebastian used it to account for "deviant" transvestism.

As Hooker comments, the major facet of etiological rhetorics is that they are useful in the construction of a coherent identity:

> The majority of those whom I have interviewed believe that they were born as homosexuals, or that familial factors operating very early in their lives determined the outcome. In any case, it is a fate over which they have no control, and in which they have no choice. It follows as a consequence that the possibility of changing to a heterosexual pattern is thought to be extremely limited. To fight against homosexuality is to fight against the inevitable, since they are fighting against their own "nature" in its essential form, as they experience it. (1967, p. 183)

The neutralization of stigma is a complex matter, and some of its elements have been clarified. First, to the legitimating knowledge of the gay world discussed in the previous chapter is added the nihilation of the straight world. All men are basically gay, and the straight world has no real existence, or at best is laughable. People considered undesirable, or not committed to the gay world, are excluded from the community, adding to the aristocratizing effect of belonging to a secret, stigmatized group. Finally, the self who experiences the neutralization of stigma is given predictability and coherence by reinterpreting his biography and setting out his future within the framework of the gay experience, by using the theories constructed by the stigmatizers themselves. Ultimately, the relationship between the stigmatizing society and those labeled deviant is encompassed by this irony.

# III. IDENTITY

# 7. IDENTITY AND SECRECY

Identity is the answer to the questions Who am I? and Where do I belong? We have examined the setting for the answers to these questions, and some modes of answering, but ultimately there is, behind each decision, a person who makes it. Both the gay community and the stigmatizing society provide definitions of what a gay person is and how to locate gayness in the self and others; identity is forged using social categories, but it is finally an individual act of faith.

SOCIETY AND STIGMA. In society as a whole, homosexual identity is imputed on the basis of homosexual acts, and social labels are attached on that basis. People labeled homosexual by police and judges are those caught in the act, often in public parks and rest rooms. People assigned to the category homosexual by social scientists doing surveys are put there because of acts. Sex with a person of the same gender is the basis of society's stigma against the homosexual, but the stigmatization process extends far beyond the sexual act to the whole life and self of the gay person.

The very fact of the deep stigma against the homosexual in our society provides him with an environment that symbolically stigmatizes even the secret homosexual who is never directly labeled by a social audience (such as the criminal justice system or straight friends and family). Symbolic stigma* comes from the mass media, from the educational system, and from casual contacts such as this:

> Sometimes I find myself drawn as into a net by the abuses and sneers of the hostile world. I hear the vile joke or the calumnious remark, and must sit in silence, or even force a smile, as it were, of approval. A passenger enters an elevator and remarks: "When I come out of a barber shop, I have a feeling I smell like a fag. I better watch out or some goddam queer'll pick me up on the way home." The operator laughs, and I find myself forcing a smile, joining in the humiliating remark, that is, unknowingly, directed against myself. (Cory, 1953, p. 11)

The symbolic stigma borne by the homosexual is based on highly negative social imagery, based on the "knowledge" of straights who, in the main, have no real knowledge of gays. As Dank (1971, p. 182) points out, only in recent years has there been some distribution of homophile material* and

---

* See Warren and Johnson (1972), for a discussion of symbolic stigma in the context of labeling theory.
* homosexual material written by homosexuals; generally ideological.

neutral (or even positive) portrayals of homosexuality in the media. The lack of positive imagery, and the corresponding absence of homosexual role models for the young, may be one reason for the typically long period of time between the first homosexual experience or feeling and the self-identification as gay—in Dank's study the average was six years (1971, p. 182).†

On the other hand, our cultural message about homosexuality is that *people who do those kinds of things are that kind of person.* In our society one can "play golf" or "be a golfer" depending on time involvement and preference, but there is no linguistic differentiation between "doing homosexual" and "being a homosexual." As a stigma, gayness is a master status; homosexuality is a "sickness" that affects the entire body, and one "deviant" act makes the social identity of the doer deviant.

As indicated, the audiences who perform actual and symbolic stigmatization are different. *Symbolic stigmatizers* are either institutional forces, like the mass media, or people who do not know that the person to whom they express their distaste for homosexuals is (or may one day be) a secret gay. *Stigmatizing audiences*, on the other hand, are those who label an overt homosexual as such, or who catch a secret homosexual in the act. As indicated in Chapter 1, that branch of deviance theory called "labeling theory" has tended to focus on just that process: stigmatization of homosexuals by the criminal justice system, which generally occurs only by catching them in the act.

Of all the homosexual acts that take place in our society, only an infinitesimally small fraction results in criminal processing; these generally are acts performed flagrantly, in front of disguised vice squad officers, in public restrooms (Gagnon and Simon, 1968). Becker and Lemert, however, in

† The term "coming out" is used in the gay community either to mean the first homosexual experience, or the first self-identification as a homosexual.

their theories of the effects of labeling and secondary deviation, place an undue amount of theoretical emphasis on
public ceremonies of degradation in the creation of a stigmatized social identity:

> One of the most crucial steps in the process of building
> a stable pattern of deviant behavior is likely to be the
> experience of being caught and publicly labeled as a de-
> viant. (Becker, 1963, p. 31)

> Secondary deviation refers to. . . essentially moral prob-
> lems which revolve around stigmatization, punishments,
> segregation, and social control. . . The secondary de-
> viant, as opposed to his actions, is a person whose life
> and identity are organized around the facts of deviance.
> (Lemert, 1967, p. 7)

These conceptions are inapplicable to the formation of
identity in the gay world for several reasons (see also Chapter
1). First, almost nobody whose "life and identity is organized
around the facts of deviance," in the context of the secret
gay community, has ever been officially stigmatized. Second,
there is nothing empirically in common among the kinds of
behavior labeled "deviant" by this theory (a mash of topics,
from jazz music to check forgery) that would warrant a
general explanatory theory of this type. And third, the theory
ignores the far more relevant processes of symbolic labeling
(already discussed), community labeling, and self-typing.


COMMUNITY AND SECRECY.   The gay community, as a
stigmatized one, provides a definition of homosexuality that
sheds stigma and adds value; as a secret community, it
provides criteria by which to recognize fellow homosexuals in
straight settings and straights who have wandered into gay

settings. The classic example of the latter is the folklore of cues for recognizing vice squad members:

> BARTENDER: I can always recognize a plainclothes vice, even if they send a new one. They look like a gay guy all right, the clothes are fine but they always forget the socks, or the shoes. Lace up shoes in a gay bar, or the wrong color socks. (Conversation)

Or the cues which signal the entry of a straight into a gay bar:

> ALPHONSE: You can tell a straight guy, he just sort of walks in and sits down, but soon he starts looking around him, staring weirdly, then he gets very fidgety, and then usually he leaves. Sometimes they get in a real panic.
>
> That's if it's an accident; if he just wants to come and gape at the queers he usually brings a girl to protect him first off, and then he sits and gapes and looks nervous, and he talks very loudly and laughs a lot. (Conversation)

In the opposite matter, recognizing homosexuality either among others or in oneself, the gay community typifies "homosexuality" and "gayness" in far more complex and rich ways than the straight community, and uses very different criteria of definition. A *homosexual identity* is distinguished from a *gay identity* by the gay community, although not by the stigmatizing society. A homosexual identity simply describes one's sexual orientation, whereas a gay identity implies affiliation with the gay community in a cultural and sociable sense. A homosexual, for the community, is one who both practices homosexuality and admits it, whereas a gay person is someone who does all that and also identifies and interacts with the gay world:

> CAROL: What do you see as a difference between "homosexual" and "gay"?
> JUSTIN: Homosexual is a sexual thing. Gay has a cultural element. (Conversation)

> CAROL: How old are you?
> JOHN: Forty.
> CAROL: Oh.
> JOHN: I started kind of late in life. Not actually started, I started rather late in life as far as leading—uh—exclusively—(pause)—homosexual—uh—not homosexual—leading the gay life, with a particular set of people I knew where just about everyone was gay. (Tape-recorded interview)

> JUSTIN: . . . most of my friends are gay, but a few are homosexual and some are straight. (Written communication)

Although this distinction was made when circumstances (or I) asked for it, the more usual practice was to use the term "gay" to designate both homosexual and gay identity, since the dichotomization of the world into straight and gay overshadows in importance the fine shades of meaning that sometimes become necessary.

The distinction between the cultural and sexual aspect of gay leaves room for an interesting possibility: a heterosexual gay. In my research I encountered one attempt at just such an identity, a self-identified heterosexual woman who constructed a gay front to ensure a welcome in a gay clique in one of the beach towns north of Sun City. This was a well-known movie star in her late fifties, several times married, who belonged to a wealthy and superannuated gay group.

She attempted to appear gay by associating with a gay-looking entourage, in particular her secretary, a very masculine-appearing woman who accompanied her everywhere. The members of her clique were ambivalent about whether she was gay. Sometimes they thought she was heterosexual but constructing a gay front, and at other times insisted that she was a lesbian and *pretending not to be by constructing a gay front.** Her own report of the situation:

> NOELLE: No, I'm not gay, I really like men. But I like gay people better than anyone, so I like to be with them.
> CAROL: They think you're gay because of Anita (the secretary). She looks so butch—and you're always together.
> NOELLE: Yes, I do that to make them feel more comfortable—Anita has a boyfriend she really likes,† but it looks better, more gay, that way. The guys really know I'm no dyke but they don't want to admit it. It makes them feel better this way. (Conversation).

Noelle and Anita later seemed to discover that the type of lesbian that would be acceptable within such a group was not the stereotype masculine butch, but rather more "feminine" women (see Chapter 5, footnote on page 133), and in a short time Anita changed her dress considerably:

> Anita has started wearing way-out clothes like Noelle, and seems to enjoy herself more. The guys were complaining that she came to parties in jeans and sweatshirts when the other gay women wore cocktail dresses, and if she wanted to dress that way she should

---

* This is similar to the report by a few secret gays that they averted the suspicion of straights by pretending or clowning at gayness.
† A gay-appearing member of Noelle's entourage.

go to the dyke bars and play pool. Maybe Noelle has
given her the word to start playing the role of the
lesbian as the group defines it, not in terms of public
stereotypes. (Field notes)

Gay identity, then, involves affiliation with the gay community, normally after the establishment of a homosexual
preference and a homosexual identity. The community
provides criteria for locating a homosexual identity that differ
from that of the stigmatizing society in that they do not
specify acts of sex, but *feelings* of romantic or emotional
sexuality as the basis of homosexuality. Whereas the process
of stigmatization by the larger society involves observation of
acts and inference of a "deviant" state of being, the gay community starts with the sense of being different and explains
the resultant acts by this essential differentness.

This means, of course, that the acts can occur without the
imputation of a homosexual essential self:

SIMEON: Lots of guys will try it once or twice if there's
nothing else around—sailors or prisoners—and they will
get sexually satisfied. But they are not homosexual, because it is not in them—they just don't feel that way for
guys, just for women.

A similar differentiation of "homosexual" from "one who is
engaging in an act for given purposes" is reported in Reiss's
study of lower-class "peers" who sell "queers" the op-
portunity to fellate them for cash. The "peers'" community
code involves the denial of romantic or sexual feeling for the
fellators; the purpose of the interaction for the boys is defined solely in terms of the money paid for services rendered
to the "deviant" queers (Reiss, 1964, pp. 113–152).

As another example, the term "bisexual" means different
things to the gay community and to the stigmatizing society.
Societally the term is used to refer to people who have sex

with people of both sexes; within the gay community, it designates a state of *being bisexual*—of feeling equally drawn to the members of both sexes, sexually and emotionally. Many times in the community I have heard the following comment made about bisexuals:

> FILMORE: You can tell a bisexual if he can't answer this question: "If a man is faced with a beautiful man and a beautiful woman, and cannot decide to whom he is most attracted, or which he would have sex with, then he is a bisexual."

This, of course, contrasts with the general societal conception, based on the sexual act: "Would you, or have you ever had, sexual relations with members of both sexes?" The gay definition of bisexuality, in fact, is the opposite to a sexual act, because it is a state of being so profoundly ambiguous that it precludes action. Furthermore, bisexuality is seen not just as bad faith but as actually impossible, since nobody, in gay folklore, could fail to make the choice between the man and the woman in such a situation, especially if he was feeling sexy.

> SIMEON: People who say they're bisexual—I don't believe them. The pendulum will always swing one way or the other. They just don't want to admit they're gay, that's all. They think it's more respectable to—that they're bisexual. (Conversation)

One flaw in labeling theory then, as indicated in Chapter 1, is that it does not take into account the labeling processes of the stigmatized group itself in providing an identity for the members, and the way these differ from the stigmatization process of the larger society. As Warren and Johnson have also shown elsewhere, labeling theory's focus on acts of deviance and acts of labeling as criteria for the taking on of a stigmatized identity and way of life are derived from the labeling theorists' use of the commonsense perspective on deviance, which in turn is the source of the criminal justice perspective—a deviant is one who does bad things (1972).*

EXISTENTIAL IDENTITY. A related critique of labeling theory is that it does not take into account self-typing or the existential aspect of the creation of identity (Rohan and Trice, 1969; Schur, 1971; Warren and Johnson, 1972). After all, it is the self who ultimately answers the questions Who am I? and Where do I belong?, and it is the self that is one of the more stubborn problems in sociological theory. The existential self (including concepts of intentionality, motive, and free will), in a discipline that deals with interaction as the basic unit of analysis, can be dealt with in one of several ways. First, it can be ignored, which is the option chosen by many statistically oriented sociologists; this option enables them to avoid the charge of "psychological reductionism."† A second possibility is identifying the self as a mirror or miniature of society, internalized within, which is the stance of symbolic interactionism. A third is the inclusion in the theory of intentionality, will, and the existential self. This option,

---

* In recent studies of stigma, my colleagues and I (including Dr. Barbara Laslett of the University of Southern California, and graduate students and research assistants Barbara Artinian, Kay Elliott, Kathie Tielmann, and Conrad Nordquist) have been engaged in the observation of various behavior changing groups, from Weight Watchers to Parents Anonymous. We have found that, in opposition to the theory of secondary deviation, negative or stigmatizing social labels may be used to *conventionalize* behavior. This also implies that behavior and identity do not necessarily vary in the same direction (see Laslett and Warren, 1973; Warren, 1973).

† There seem to be two major negative insult labels in academic sociology with which to insult one's opponents: "psychological reductionism" and "armchair sociology."

which is mine, presents methodological difficulty in inferring intention and other existential states from behavior and conversation (see Appendix).

The identity of the gay individual (or any other, I believe) is *not determined*, either by social stigma or the labels of the gay community. Identity is an existential choice belonging to the self, using the available social meanings in a unique and personal way. For one thing, the meanings themselves may contain ambivalences and difficulties that require interpretation; even stigmatization has loopholes. For example, the person who ultimately chooses a gay identity learns during socialization that homosexuality is defined by sexual acts with members of the same sex, *but* that these acts represent a complete social identity. He is taught that homosexuality is bad and so are homosexuals, *but* he is taught to recognize homosexuals by lurid signs such as extreme effeminacy or a fiendish, warped, or debauched appearance (thus he is not equipped to recognize actual homosexuals). These rather confusing elements that make up the societal stereotype of homosexuals actually provide a homosexual actor with ways out of self-labeling as a homosexual. For one thing, he can conclude that despite sexual acts he cannot be a homosexual, since he has learned that homosexuals are recognizably weird looking, and he is not:

> ELDON: I had been told by my mother that all fairies as she called them were very light and small and I was big and muscular so I knew I wasn't one.

The negative definition of homosexuality may belie the experience:

> DRUMMOND: As far as I knew homosexuality was a horrible thing, and I knew sex with Gerald was fantastic, so I knew I couldn't be homosexual.

Finally, if his social identity is heterosexual, homosexual acts may be neutralized as accidents of fate:

> BRUCE: I was engaged to be married, so every time me and my college roommate made it we said "Boy was I drunk last night" and left it at that. (Conversation)

In any case, stigmatization or public labeling tends to be less significant in the choice of gay identity than interaction with the gay community. In Dank's study of coming out into homosexual identity, (1971), there were no cases where performance of homosexual acts stimulated self-identification, and only a few members reported labeling by officials of social control. Other societal sources of self-definition included reading about homosexuality (15%), being fired from a job because of homosexual imputations (1%), imprisonment or mental hospitalization (3%), and seeing a psychiatrist or professional counselor (5%) (Dank, 1971, p. 187). Both in this study and in Dank's, most "coming outs" occurred in the context of interaction with other gays (in Dank's study the figure was 50%). Although nearly all the members had had homosexual experience before they had any contact with the community, the identity phase of coming out happened in the gay world, partly because of two related factors: the conversion effect and the impact of the community as an institution.

The conversion effect starts with what has been called the "phenomenological shock" of encountering a stigmatized group and finding that they appear "normal" and are not distinguished by bizarre physical markings or extraordinary appearance and behavior. Such a shock happens to many people, especially to those whose job takes them into contact with the stigmatized: police officers, sociologists, and journalists. Many gay people reported experiencing this kind of shock:

BINGHAM: One time out of curiosity I went to a gay bar to see what these freaks really looked like. It really hit me. They looked just like me! I couldn't imagine what I was going to find in there, but I knew it was going to be weird. And it wasn't weird. Most of them were just regular guys. One of the guys picked me up and we went home together. (Conversation)

When shock is added to previous homosexual interests and activities, the possibility of conversion becomes a very real one, once again highlighting the irony that stigmatization can, in less direct ways than labeling theory implies, promote affiliation with the stigmatized group. The shock of normalcy would not be possible if the learning of bizarreness had not preceded it.

The effect of the community itself on identity choice has become cumulatively clear in the preceding chapters. Stigmatization and secrecy, the closing in of the community as the centrally defining aspect of life, the spending of leisure in highly structured (indeed institutionalized) gay settings and interactions, and the development of gay relationships all promote affiliation and identification with the community, underpinned by the learning of a new world of knowledge.* Yet even this is not enough to *determine* identity:

> Noreen met Viva at work, and Viva invited her away for a weekend and tried to seduce her. Viva had been a committed member of the gay community for around twenty years, but Noreen had had no homosexual experience or contact with the gay community, and at first was shocked, and cried. After a time, Viva invited Noreen for a second weekend, during which they became sexually involved. The pair lived together for ten

---

* A final factor in this summation, of course, is the homosexual desire itself.

years, during which they were almost entirely immersed in the gay community in their leisure orientation, and did not date men. Noreen agreed that she was sexually and romantically involved with Viva, was "in love with" her (meeting both societal and gay community criteria of homosexuality), but insisted that she was "basically heterosexual." The gay community of which she was a part claimed that she was deluding herself, and was basically not only gay but butch-aggressive. Noreen claimed that her relationship with Viva was unique and a once-only thing, and that if it broke up she would go with a man. Eventually, Viva went out with other women, and Noreen broke off the ten-year relationship. Within a few weeks, Noreen had found a steady boyfriend and had severed some ties with the gay community. After a few months she had severed almost all ties, and was deeply involved with the boyfriend. (Case history summary)

This is a unique case in my experience, but less dramatic instances are more frequent. It is not rare, for example, to find people who are willing to accept a homosexual identity but not a gay identity, generally because of some critical attitude toward the culture with which that identity is associated. Some men regard the gay community as too isolated from the rest of the world; others, like gay liberationists, regard it as too secretive. Still others see it as culturally impoverished and intellectually arid (see also Gagnon and Simon, 1968), and some do not like the stigma attached to membership in the community and remain "closet queens," either alone or with a lover. A few, like Jason, just don't like to be pinned down and labeled by others, and resist self-labeling:

> CAROL: How do you conceive of yourself?
> JASON: Mostly in terms of—er—you know—not so much of broad categories like gay or straight or student

but really in terms of what I am—in terms of, you know, more of my uniqueness, rather than in more of my general features.

CAROL: Do you think that's realistic?

JASON: What do you mean realistic?

CAROL: I knew you would say that. Do you think that if you gave that answer to members of society they would accept it?

JASON: Well—people, you know, when people first meet each other they usually talk about themselves in terms of—you know—what broad categories they fit into, but—that isn't the same thing as saying how do I conceive of myself.

CAROL: If someone asked you if you were gay or straight, what would you say?

JASON: It would depend on who was asking me.

CAROL: At a party, say.

JASON: At a gay party?

CAROL: A stranger. At a gay party.

JASON: Oh, I would say I was gay.

CAROL: What would you say at a straight party?

JASON: Well, I would say I wasn't, I guess.

CAROL: Well, what you're saying is you use these categories in interacton but you don't use them in your self-image.

JASON: Right, this is a duality. (Tape-recorded interview)

These rare cases of rejection of gay identity within the context of the gay community are important not just as negative cases but because they highlight a universal process, the formation of self-identification as a choice—a single choice in a lifetime, a process or self-identification that takes a lifetime, or any variation in between. In deterministic models such as labeling theory, anomie theory, and subcultural theory, people's identity is seen as determined by one or another aspect of the social system; in labeling theory it is others' labels, in subcultural theory it is being born into an alternative value system, and in anomie theory it is victimization by an anomic society. The existential perspective recognizes the impact of all relevant social circumstances on identity, but asserts that the identity generated is not determined by these circumstances. Clearly, there are similarities of experiencing stigmatization and interaction with the gay community. In addition to these structural similarities, there are some existential similarities.

Many members reported symbolic aspects of their conversion not related directly to community or stigma, but rather to a kind of universal human confrontation of self, alone or with others. In quite a few instances this took a sexual form:

> JEREMIAH: For years I was just trade,* wouldn't put one of those dirty things in my mouth. Look what I was missing. (Conversation)

> SIMEON: Lots of men who are straight and do the scene sometimes for fun, they'd do anything for you, but not kiss you on the mouth. That's what they do with their wife. (Conversation)

These and many similar comments indicate the importance of the sexual kiss as an experience that generates gay identity, a theme repeated throughout the literature but never quite understood in its existential significance. Like Reiss's peers, many men who are willing to be fellated by other men will not give the genital kiss with their own mouths in return; when they do, this can provide the final experience of identification. The mouth kiss is similar, perhaps even more a sym-

---

* Indicates a male willing to be fellated by other males but not willing to reciprocate.

bol of gayness, since males in our society are freer to be sexual than to be tender:

> BINGHAM: I had sex with guys and it felt good. But that's as far as it went—it was sort of I'll scratch your back and you'll scratch mine. But I never would have thought of kissing a man—on the mouth, that is—that would have been an expression of feeling, and would have revolted me—when I finally did kiss a guy romantically, I realized that I was a homosexual. (Conversation)

## THE EXPERIENCE OF GAY IDENTITY.

Donald Webster Cory has provided a vivid expression of the experience of being gay:

> Fundamental to all answers is an understanding that the dominant factor in my life, towering in importance above all others, is a consciousness that I am different. In one all-important respect, I am unlike the great mass of people always around me, and the knowledge of that fact is with me at all times, influencing profoundly my every thought, each minute activity, and all my aspirations. It is inescapable, not only this being different but this constant awareness of a dissimilarity.... An insatiable curiosity grips me as I yearn to know what it would be like not to be a homosexual.... But it is all in vain. It is outside the realm of my wildest flights of fancy. I am powerless even to capture a dream image of another world...a state of existence in which I would be like others is utterly beyond my conception. (1953, p. 7)

> *I am different.* I am different from all these people, and I must always be different from them. I do not belong to them nor they to me. (1953, p. 9)

Although of course the essence of the experience varies for each individual, there are certain generalities that describe the experience of being gay, once gay identity is chosen. Although there are many aspects of this experience, perhaps the most important elements are totality, belonging, and distinction.

*Totality.*   The gay world, because it is stigmatized and set apart, is one that demands total identification. Thus a person who affiliates with the community and accepts gay identity possesses a rarity in contemporary life: a total and all-encompassing core of existence by which to answer the question Who am I?

Most people today, if one considers the vast literature on alienation and the search for identity as a criterion, have no clear answer to that question. Unless they belong to a group which is somehow set apart from the mainstream of society (such as Negroes, Mexican Americans, and women), and unless that difference is consciously expressed as identity (blacks, Chicanos, and feminists), there is no anchorage for identity as there was in the stable social world of traditional society. As Cory says, in the anonymity of urban society "In one all-important respect I am unlike the great mass of people always around me."

*Belonging.*   With the experience of totality comes the sense of belonging to and with those who are the same, an answer to the question Where do I belong? This closeness, again, becomes a crucial experience only when it is conscious, that is, only when the positive aspects of belonging to the group override the pain of stigmatization. Blacks who are "Step'n'fetchit," Mexicans who feel inferior to Anglos, and gays who think they are sick and sinful cannot experience the benefits of belonging or the comfort of their stigmatized identity.

As Simmel so perceptively saw, secrecy adds fatefulness to belonging and totality, and it draws the community in upon itself as a major resource and motive in the members' lives. Cory, who as a married man chose exclusion from the sociable community of the gay world, experienced the secrecy but not the brotherhood, thus Terrence says it better:

> The gay world *is* the world as far as I'm concerned. I belong with people like me, and I have nothing in common with the others, and I don't associate with them any more. (Conversation)

*Distinction.* As Terrence's statement implies, belonging involves distinction, both in its positive and negative aspects. Cory adds: "I am different from all these people, and I must always be different from them. I do not belong to them, nor they to me." Negatively, distinction from others can bring alienation and even open conflict between people who might otherwise have been allies: friends, family, workmates. Even when straight people are unaware of others' being gay, and thus do not stigmatize them, the fear of discrediting leads gay people to stay aloof and distinct from the lives and involvements of others. For some this can be experienced as distress, although others either do not care or learn not to care.

When secrecy is added to distinction, there is the nagging fear of exposure, to which is added the constant interactional schizophrenia of those who pretend to an identity that they do not have or leave unsaid an identity that is fundamental to them. Again, although some did not complain about this split and others judged it fun, many found it to be both painful and troublesome.

One positive aspect of such switching, of course, is what Berger (1963) calls the experience of ecstasy. Ecstasy is both the ability to take the world as problematic rather than for granted and the ability to switch roles with great facility and legitimacy. Gay people get to do both very well, like good sociologists, plainclothes detectives, and conpersons. Other positive aspects of distinction, stigmatization, and secrecy have already been discussed: the sense of membership in an elect group, the warmth of belonging, and the security of a clear self-definition.

Above all, gay identity is distinct. It sets the experience of being gay apart from the experience of life in mass society, and by that alone makes the gay world a kind of haven. It provides a clear answer to the questions Who am I? and Where do I belong? The gay community provides a choice of distinction in mass society and will, for that, endure all kinds of social storms—except, perhaps, the end of stigmatization and the end of secrecy.

# APPENDIX. METHODS OF RESEARCH

To approach existential understanding of a world framed through the meanings the members give to it requires observation and participation. Presented as a continuum, observation is the viewing of the world from a distance, as a whole from the outside, like the astronauts' photographs of the earth taken from outer space, whereas participation is unreflective immersion in that world, without a total picture, distance, or thought.

As these analogies indicate, pure types of observation and participation are ideal types, and not realities. The astronauts' view of the world is not actually objective, since they grew up in that world, and the meanings of that world frame their view of it, even from the outer space. As the imaginatively named "Martian method" of pure observation indicates, only

Martians (not humans) could observe human reality without using human subjective meanings. From the same
perspective, pure participational subjectivity is also impossible, since human beings use language, which catego-
rizes and sorts information at the moment of experiencing it.
Even the most complete participant remains partially an observer; even the most subjective observer remains clearly a
subjective participant.

Participant observation, or field research, as a method of
the social sciences involves *reflective subjectivity* as a
perspective and immersion into the actor's social world as a
tool. Reflective subjectivity acknowledges the humanness of
the sociologist while increasing the reflective observation of
everyday life through special training and special tools such
as field notes and interviews.

Entering the setting as an actor allows to the sociologist
both existential freedom and sometimes painful constraint.
The constraint resides in the fact that the observer may have
to lay aside her prejudices and fears, likes and dislikes, an-
noyances and timidities, and approach people and situations
within the setting that seem unappealing, hostile, or inac-
cessible.* The freedom is intrinsic to being an actor on the
social scene, and it means that all data are fundamentally a
product of the human ways of gathering and interpreting
them.†

ENTERING THE WORLD.    The gay world had opened for
me some time before I wrote this book, so entree was not a
problem—those readers interested in hints on initial entree
must look elsewhere (e.g., Lofland, 1972; Schatzman and

* If the whole setting seems that way, it is a bad idea to do research in it.
† This, of course, is the major argument of the ethnomethodologists (see
Garfinkel, 1967; Cicourel, 1964).

Strauss, 1973, 18–32; Johnson, 1971). But the experience of entering settings is repeated time and time again in the study of a community, since the sociologist's task involves the facing of new situations, new problems, and new faces (other members may be quite content with a stable circle of a few acquaintances and a strictly limited place round).

One problem is what John Johnson (1971) calls "the line of least resistance." Especially in the gay community, where the focus is on fun and sociability, it was frequently difficult for me to persuade myself to have less fun than everyone else by talking to people I didn't like, or not drinking so that I could concentrate better. Sometimes I persuaded, sometimes I didn't.

It is not always a case of the line of least resistance, either; certain parts of setting may remain unentered for better reasons. As a woman studying a predominantly male gay community, there were places I could not go that might have relevance for my study: tearooms, Turkish baths, or YMCA locker rooms. Furthermore, there were other settings I could enter, but not without radically changing their character. One example that springs to mind is cliques or pairs of male homosexuals who uncompromisingly detest women. If a woman gains access to such a clique, she has already changed its character.

Contrary to popular sterotype, I encountered only a few such cliques. In one large cocktail party, with about seventy men and a few women present, I noticed that a couple of men were studiously avoiding me, to the point of moving to the other side of the room whenever I was in the vicinity. I asked the host who they were, and he said they were a wealthy couple from San Francisco who "really hate women and never have anything to do with them, socially or ever, so I had better not go up and speak to them." Of course, after a couple of fortifying drinks, I attempted to strike up a conversation, which went something like this:

> CAROL: Hello, I'm Carol.
> TED: I'm Ted, and this is Jim. (Silence.)
> CAROL: I hear you're just down from San Francisco?
> TED: Yes.
> CAROL: How do you like Sun City?
> TED: I don't.
> CAROL: Oh? Not even our beaches?
> TED: Excuse me. We must be going. (Ted and Jim move to the other side of the room.)

The conversation had a kind of stony horror not reproducible on paper. Later I learned that Ted and Jim live in a gay world of wealthy men who don't work and are able to disassociate themselves entirely from women. By definition, I could never study such a world.

Another kind of problem sometimes occurs when community members know that a sociologist is doing research— they put you on. This is not a problem confined to prostitute respondents who are paid for giving data and feel they have to give the poor john a really good story. Especially in a community where sociability is the main activity, and putting people on is one of the happenings, this can happen very often, and certainly happened to me from time to time:

> Gene said to me in conversation at the bar this evening: "There was this guy from Local College doing research as he called it, and he was really gorgeous, really groovy and straight. Well, we all really gave him a bad time, told him all of these things, like we used bananas up our ass, and he wrote it all down—for weeks, it was fun." I asked Gene why it was fun, and he indicated that it provided a change from the same old routine at the bar.

> Alex told me with a straight face this evening that he and Jake get their kicks sitting on their roof with raincoats and boots on. I saw a certain gleam in his eye

when he said it, and he added: "Tell that when you write your book." (Field notes)

Problems of the line of least resistance and its opposite can be multiplied by other types of problem, but that is not necessary. These examples indicate that there is really no such thing as "entering the community" once and for all; instead, there is a continuing process of making and breaking contacts, and making and breaking relationships, in which tactics rather than strategies are of the most help.

RULES AND ROLES. The difference between strategies and tactics may be summarized as follows: A strategy calls for an overall plan of action with attendant abstract contingencies, whereas tactics are the actions taken to implement that plan in the field. The literature of participant observation, as of other sociological methodologies, is full of strategies or rules (the most comprehensive of which are the stage theories of field research; see Becker, 1970, pp. 228–244, for an example).

One set of rules concerns the taking and playing of a role by the observer. Almost inevitably, the researcher is exhorted to decide on a particular role to play in the setting—covert or overt—and play it.* This abstract type of rule, however, ignores the situational and interpretive nature of social interaction. Most generally, in some settings (perhaps the board room of a large corporation) the identity of a stranger will come into question, whereas in other settings (such as a gay party full of strangers to one another) it may not.

Rules about choosing and playing a role ignore interactional contingencies as well as general differences between

---

* I fell victim to this dichotory in the first phase of my methods (see Warren, 1972).

settings. In an early stage of this research,I had the following
conversation: *

> CAROL: I'm here to do some sociological research on
> the gay world.
> MICHAEL: Oh come now, I've heard it all.
> CAROL: Really, that's what I'm doing.
> MICHAEL: Knew a priest once, said he was in the bars
> to save men's souls but all I ever saw him doing was
> feeling them up in the head.† Now I know some nice
> girls you might like . . . .

In general, the role chosen and played emerges from the
interaction, not vice versa. What is more, roles are ne-
gotiated, not chosen by the sociologist as this interchange
suggests. A researcher may define herself as just about
anything, but the members may insist that she is a vice
squad member, a latent homosexual, a closet case, a nosy
person getting kicks, and so on. I learned to let the other
person do my defining for me, and made an effort to ne-
gotiate a particular role only when data gathering demanded
it. To get interviews, for example, I had to mention that I was
a sociologist, since this was not an activity typical of fag
hags, lesbians, nosy people getting kicks, or even police officers.

To restate: I am defining the problem of role playing as a
practical, tactical, and interactional one, not as a strategic,
abstract, or even ethical one.‡ Another practical problem, I
found, was deciding where to go and who to affiliate with.
The gay community is made up of multiple cliques, whose
members shift and change, and which do not necessarily get

---

* A graduate student at USC, Barbara Ponse, has found the same kind of
disbelief in her study of overt lesbian activities.
† This is an inadvertent double or triple pun: a head is a restroom and also
several parts of the body in various kinds of dialect.
‡ Within, of course, the general ethic of doing no harm to subjects.

along with one another. I could either drift around trying not to become affiliated with anyone in particular (and thus probably get nowhere), or affiliate with a definite circle (and get ostracized from some others). I took a middle-range approach most of the time. I got to know several cliques quite well, but kept some distance from them in order to move into other situations. I also became something of a "star," attracting members to myself and the people I knew.* Sometimes these tactics were successful, and at other times they did not do as well:

> Dick called me up and invited me to go to Beach Town for Sunday brunch with that new set of "wealthy queens" he's always talking about, so of course I accepted. Justin called almost immediately afterward and suggested that "our group" get together for Sunday brunch, since he wanted me to meet some friends of his from out of town. I knew that Justin resented Dick's defection from "the crowd" so I indicated unspecifically that I had another engagement, which bugged him. But he did suggest Saturday night dinner instead, which I accepted.
>
> Joe, I hear, has been commenting to some of his friends: "Carol's too good for us now, she's always up at Beach City carrying on with those rich bitches up there." When I called and invited him over, he was quite cold and claimed he had something planned "every weekend for the next three months." (Field notes)

Where to go is an ecological as well as a relational problem. As I got to know more people I was invited to more and more homes, often at the same time, and had to weigh

---

* This experience is quite common in field research: researchers are such good listeners, and so genuinely interested in others. Barbara Ponse again had a similar experience studying the female gays. (See also Schatzman and Strauss, 1973).

increasingly carefully the question of where to go, making sure that I didn't always go where it would be most fun, where everybody liked me, or where I felt most at home. Since there were only thirteen bars in the city, and I couldn't go into the famous Turkish baths, routine bargoing was no problem; however, where to go was a problem on ritual occasions like Halloween. Generally, I did what the members did at such times, and crammed in as many of the drag contests and bars as possible on the two Halloweens I had.

It is my contention that the research process in the field is much more fluid, ambiguous, tactical, and problematic than strategic, abstract, or predictable. The actual behavior characterizing reflective subjectivity might best be described as a kind of *disciplined living*, which gave way sometimes on the discipline and sometimes on the living. Sometimes I entered situations where I didn't feel researcher-ish, or emotions got out of hand, or maybe I started unreflective but then got my sociological imagination stirred up by some event or comment. In any case, sometimes subjectivity and experience took primacy over thought:

> I started to quizz Jeremiah about his political beliefs, mainly to find out more about what I had observed to be the great conservatism of the gay community. He expressed a few prejudices that shook me up, and I found myself quite irascible on the subject of prejudice and sociological research. Later, I realized that I had stopped listening to him at about that point, and had been overcome by my own rhetoric. (Field notes)

At other times, I would rather have done something different, but a dogged sense of research discipline made me hang in there:

> I met an interesting zoologist at Jake's party, and we discussed his job for a while. Then he made some com-

ment about being into the sadomasochistic scene, which I felt obliged to follow up, although right then I was much more interested in zoology. (Field notes)

Mostly what I did was live—make friends, join cliques, go to parties, laugh, argue, drink, go to the beach—while trying to remain sociologically reflective not just as an actor on the social scene, but an analyzer, noter, prodder, and prober of it. I discovered that there was no problem of either being or going native in the gay world and forgetting to take that world as problematic; gay people are naturally immersed in the sociological perspective, because secrecy requires that they be competent actors and minute analysts of social nuances (see also Humphreys, 1972, pp. 168–172). Like sociologists, gay people consciously define gay and straight, learn the meaning of a presentation of self, and achieve role distance. In this sense, "going native" in the gay world would involve some of the same kinds of mental gymnastics as going native in the sociologists' world.

INTERVIEWS. As Becker comments, some generalizations about a given world are observed and deduced, whereas others may be confirmed by the members themselves, or disconfirmed, either voluntarily or in response to a direct question (1970, pp. 405–406). Interviews can be used to test observations in this way and for other purposes—to discover new theoretical directions, to check the effects on the members' world of doing research (and their ideas about "what sociology is"), and to keep some of my data in permanent, uncollaped form on tapes, for future reference.

The process of questioning and answering that goes on in interviewing can have all kinds of ramifications. Observed generalities can be bolstered comfortably, or shattered; new possibilities may be created. One example of the latter oc-

curred to me in connection with the etiology of homosexuality. Both myself as a sociologist and the members
as competent social actors knew that interviews involved
questioning and answering; so far we agreed. But, also as
competent social actors who "knew" that social research
means investigating causes of deviant behavior, they were, as
far as I was concerned, dead wrong.

At first, I discounted as irrelevant, dead data the long
stories members gave me about "how they got that way,"
since I had learned not to cut them off short when they got
into that topic. Soon, however, I realized that these tales had
considerable uniformity, and they tallied well with all kinds of
deterministic social science theories of dominant mothers,
environment, traumas, seduction, and other assorted things.
It occurred to me, as I have described more fully in Chapter
6, that these social science rhetorics were being put to good
use in the construction of members' current identifies and
commitments.

I was glad, then, that I had preserved so many hours of
etiological theory. Some of these raw data, however, become less meaningful (and even meaningless) outside the
context in which they were expressed. For example, at the
time this statement was made I knew what it meant, but
having played and replayed it since, I have no idea what
Lonny is saying:

> CAROL: Have you ever been married?
> LONNY: No, never.
> CAROL: What has prevented you?*
> LONNY: First of all, the dumbness of a woman.
> CAROL: What does that mean?
> LONNY: Well, maybe its only my past experiences.

* The apparent dumbness of this question to a male homosexual is because of a previous comment by Lonny that he liked females sexually as
well as men.

Explaining, explaining everything, other than, such as—
um—being with the person myself alone I think that
they should know how to act with every type of person,
whether its good or bad, farmer or banker, straight or
gay person, be themselves, voice their own opinion, and
in certain circumstances alone and many times not
when its called for them to—um—voice their opinion
with another woman. Other than that—um—be so
subtle in their opinion, to me, call me down if I ask to
be. So many do not. They are like a duck that water
goes off their back and—well, forget it. (Tape-recorded
interview)

Interviews tend to reveal how the members see sociology
and sociologists. I have already shown how they view the sociological task as the investigation of the etiology of deviance. Another stereotype of the sociologist I encountered
was that sociologists are public relations persons for deviants, combating the prevailing stereotypes of homosexuals
as effeminate, child molesters, and dirty old men. However,
at least a few people regarded this kind of stereotype
destruction as dangerous to secrecy:

> JUSTIN: You had better not go around letting people
> know the stereotypes aren't true. They will be coming
> around taking another look at people like me. (Con-
> versation)

In a book concerned with identity—which is a very personal thing—interviews also serve to get a sense of the
unique individual, with a unique biography, experience of the
world, and conception of self. This was most important in
Chapter 7 of the book, where I consider the formation of
identity in the context of cues from the secret gay community
and the stigmatizing society. Such data always, however,
present an ultimate problem of interpretation. We know that

people reinterpret their biographies from the standpoint of their (new) present selves; thus we can never be sure of the reality base of the biographies of identity that people give us. Perhaps, though, what is important is the reconstruction itself, and the way it organizes the past, present, and future of the self into a coherent identity.

DOCUMENTS.    Goffman has said that the stigmatized inhabit a literally defined world (1963). Although many of the people I studied did read gay literature, it was mainly of the pornographic sort; although they read mass media renditions of the gay world, it was generally by chance rather than design. Therefore, I have used gay documents as evidence only for comparative purposes in Chapter 5, to contrast the secret gay community with the overt political-activist type described by Humphreys (1970; 1972), which is a much *more* literarily defined world, making the usual kinds of political use out of journals, pamphlets, newspapers, and other paper. Of this community, members may sometimes pick up a copy of the *Advocate* (the largest gay newspaper) or the *California Scene* (a rather conservative glossy) or free bar guides and advertising sheets like *Action Magazine*. But they are not likely to take a subscription; this is secrecy's anathema. I have thus made only small use of written material for this book.

DATA    PRESENTATION.    The quotes from interviews, field notes, case studies, and gay documents are used in three ways. In most cases, the data are used to support the discussion of the gay community and world, illustrating general observations with specific examples representative of many examples. In the discussion of identity, particularly in the last two chapters, the data are used to highlight the biographical experiences of members as they relate to stigmatization and resocialization. Finally, data sometimes are used to illustrate negative instances; this use has been noted carefully in the text. The aware reader will notice a considerable number of quotes from a taped interview with John. I found that John was what the anthropologists call a key informant on the gay community, putting into thoughtful and insightful words what some of the others put into less complex form. So rather than quote them, I have quoted extensively from him.

Sometimes I refer to the work of other sociologists, either theorists like Simmel, Goffman, and Lyman and Scott, or people who have written on methodology such as Lofland, Strauss and Schatzman, or other analysts of the gay community, particularly Hooker, Dank, and Simon and Gagnon. I quote the other gay studies to illustrate important convergences and divergences with mine, and the theorists and methodologies to indicate continuities and generalities in sociological theorizing, and my own particular conceptual and theoretical background.

In the final analysis, however, this book is mine; my (trained sociological) presentation of the world as I sub-jectively and reflectively experienced it, with the cooperation of the people who have been transformed, by methodology, into the somewhat dry category of data. I hope that both their voices and mine speak through the data to the existential humanity we all share.

BIBLIOGRAPHY

Achilles, Nancy, "The Development of the Homosexual Bar as an Institution," in *Sexual Deviance*, John H. Gagnon and William Simon, Eds., New York: Harper and Row, 1967, pp. 228–244.

*The Advocate*, **4**:24, January 20–Feburary 2, 1971.

Becker, Howard S., *Outsiders*, Glencoe, Ill.: Free Press, 1963.

Berger, Peter L. *Invitation to Sociology: A Humanistic Perspective*, New York: Anchor Books, 1963.

Berger, Peter L., and Thomas Luckmann, *The Social Construction of Reality*, Garden City, N.Y.: Doubleday, 1967.

Bergler, Edmund, *One Thousand Homosexuals*, Paterson, N.J.: Pageant Books, 1959.

Blumer, Herbert, "Society as Symbolic Interaction," in *Symbolic Interaction: A Reader in Social Psychology*, Jerome G. Manis and Bernard N. Meltzer, Eds., Boston: Allyn and Bacon, 1967, pp. 139–148.

*California Scene*, **1**:9, October 1970.

Cavan, Sherri, *Liquor License*, Chicago: Aldine, 1965.

Cicourel, Aaron, V., *Method and Measurement in Sociology*, New York: Free Press, 1964.

Cooley, Charles Horton, "Looking Glass Self," in *A Reader in Social Psychology*, Jerome G. Manis and Bernard N. Meltzer, Eds:, Boston: Allyn and Bacon, 1967, pp, 231–234.

Cory, Donald Webster, *The Homosexual in America*, New York: Greenberg, 1951.

Dank, Barry, "Coming Out in the Gay Community," *Psychiatry*, **34**, May 1971.

Douglas, Jack D., *American Social Order*, New York: Free Press, 1971.

Durkheim, Emil, *The Division of Labor in Society*, Glencoe, Ill.: Free Press, 1960.

Emerson, Joan, "Nothing Unusual is Happening," in *Human Nature & Collective Behavior*. Shibutani Tamotsu, Eds., Englewood Cliffs, N.J.: Prentice Hall, 1970, pp. 208–222.

Epstein, Joseph, "Homo/Hetero: The Struggle for Sexual Identity," *Harper's Magazine*, **241**: 1444, September 1970, pp. 37–51.

Erikson, Kai, T., *Wayward Puritans, a Study in the Sociology of Deviance*, New York: John Wiley, 1966.

*Exodus*, **1**:1, October 4, 1970.

Gagnon, John M., and William Simon, "Homosexuality: The Formulation of a Sociological Perspective," in *Approaches to Deviance: Theories, Concepts and Research Findings,* Mark Lefton, James K. Skipper, Jr., and Charles H. McGaghy, Eds., New York: Appleton-Century-Crofts, 1968, pp. 349–361.

Garfinkel, Harold, *Studies in Ethnomethodology*, Englewood Cliffs, N.J., Prentice-Hall, 1967.

Geddes, Donald Porter, *An Analysis of the Kinsey Reports of Sexual Behavior in the Human Male and Female*, New York: E. P. Dutton, 1953.

Glaser, Barney G., and Anselm L. Strauss, *The Discovery of Grounded Theory: Strategies for Qualitative Research,* Chicago: Aldine, 1967.

Goffman, Erving, *The Presentation of Self in Everyday Life*, New York: Anchor Books, 1959.

Goffman, Erving, *Stigma: Notes on the Management of Spoiled Identity*, Englewood Cliffs, N.J.: Prentice-Hall, 1963.

Hoffman, Martin, *The Gay World*, New York: Basic Books, 1968.

Hooker, Evelyn, "Male Homosexuality," in *Taboo Topics*, Norman L. Farberow, Ed., New York: Atherton Press, 1963, pp. 44–55.

Hooker, Evelyn, "Male Homosexuals and their 'Worlds,'" in *Sexual Inversion*, Judd Marmor, Ed., New York: Basic Books, 1965, pp. 83–105.

Hooker, Evelyn, "The Homosexual Community," in *Sexual Deviance*, John H. Gagnon and William Simon, Eds., New York: Harper and Row, 1967, pp. 167–184.

Humphreys, Laud, *Tearoom Trade: Impersonal Sex in Public Places*, Chicago: Aldine, 1970.

Humphreys, Laud, "New Styles in Homosexual Manliness," *Trans-Action*, March-April, 1971, pp. 36–46ff.

Humphreys, Laud, *Out of the Closets: the Sociology of Homosexual Liberation*, Englewood Cliffs, N.J.: Prentice-Hall, 1972.

Jackson, Dan, "*What is Male Heterosexuality?*", Bay Area Reporter, 2:3, February 1, 1970.

Johnson, John M., "Doing Field Work," unpublished manuscript, 1971.

Karlen, Arno, *Sexuality and Homosexuality: a New View*, New York: W. W. Norton, 1971.

Kinsey, A. C., et al., *Sexual Behavior in the Human Male*, Philadelphia: Saunders, 1948.

Kitsuse, John I., "Social Reactions to Deviant Behavior: Problems of Theory and Methods," in *The Other Side*, Howard S. Becker, Ed., New York: Free Press, 1964, pp. 87–102.

Laslett, Barbara, and Carol A. B. Warren, "Losing Weight. Organizational Strategies for Behavior Change," paper read at the Pacific Sociological Association annual meeting, Tempe, Ariz., May, 1973.

Lemert, Edwin, *Human Deviance, Social Problems, and Social Control*, Englewood Cliffs, N.J.: Prentice-Hall, 1967.

Leznoff, Maurice, and William Westley, "The Homosexual Community," in *Sexual Deviance*, John H. Gagnon and William Simon, Eds., New York, Harper and Row, 1967, pp. 184–196.

Livingood, John M., NIMH Task Force on Homosexuality: *Final Report and Background Papers*, Maryland: NIMH, 1972.

Lofland, John, *Analyzing Social Settings*, Belmont, Calif.: Wadsworth, 1970.

Lofland, John, *Deviance and Identity*, Englewood Cliffs, N.J.: Prentice-Hall, 1969.

Lyman, Stanford M. and Marvin Scot, *A Sociology of the Absurd*, New York: Appleton-Century-Crofts, 1970.

Lynd, Helen Merrill, *On Shame and the Search for Identity*, London: Routledge and Kegan Paul, 1958.

Magee, Bryan, *One in Twenty*, New York: Stein and Day, 1966.

Matza, David, *Becoming Deviant*, Englewood Cliffs, N.J.: Prentice-Hall, 1969.

May, Rollo, Ernest Angel, and Henri F. Ellenberger, Eds., *Existence: A New Dimension in Psychiatry and Psychology*, New York: Basic Books, 1958.

McIntosh, Mary, "The Homosexual Role," *Social Problems*, **16**:2, Fall, 1968.

Meltzer, Bernard N., "Mead's Social Psychology," in *A Reader in Social Psychology, Symbolic Interaction:* Jerome G. Manis and Bernard N. Meltzer, Eds., Boston: Allyn and Bacon, 1967, pp. 5–24.

Miller, Merle, *On Being Different: What It Means to Be a Homosexual*, New York: Random House, 1971.

*The Prodigal,* **2**:22, April 18, 1971.

Reiss, Albert J., "The Social Integration of Queers and Peers," in *The Other Side*, Howard S. Becker, Ed., New York: Free Press, 1964, pp. 113–152.

Rohan, Paul M., and Harrison M. Trice, "The Self Reaction: A Neglected Dimension of Labeling Theory," unpublished paper, 1969.

Ross, H. Laurence, "Modes of Adjustment of Married Homosexuals," *Social Problems,* **18**:3, Winter, 1971, pp. 385–393.

Rubington, Earl, and Martin S. Weinberg, "Deviant Identity," in *Deviance: The Interactionist Perspective*, Earl Rubington and Martin S. Weinberg, Eds., New York: Macmillan, 1968, pp. 318–321.

Schatzman, Leonard, and Anselm, L. Strauss, *Field Research: Strategies for a Natural Sociology*, Englewood Cliffs, N.J.: Prentice-Hall, 1973.

Scheff, Thomas, *Being Mentally Ill*, Chicago: Aldine, 1966.

Schofield, Michael, *Sociological Aspects of Homosexuality*, Boston: Little, Brown and Co., 1965.

Schur, Edwin M., *Labeling Deviant Behavior*, New York: Harper and Row, 1971.

Schutz, Alfred, *Collected Papers, Vol. 1: The Problem of Social Reality*, The Hague: Martinus Nijhoff, 1970.

Simmel, Georg, *The Sociology of Georg Simmel*, Kurt H. Wolff, Ed. and Trans., Glencoe, Ill.: Free Press, 1950.

Simon, William, and John H. Gagnon, "Femininity in the Lesbian Community," in *Social Problems*, Fall, 1967, **15**:2, pp. 212–221.

Starr, Michael, "Straight or Not, Many Authors have made the Stage a Little Gayer," in *The Advocate*, **4**:24, January 20–February 2, 1971, p. 10.

Sykes, Gresham M., *The Society of Captives*, Princeton, N.J.: Princeton University Press, 1968.

Warren, Carol A. B., "Observing the Gay Community," in *Research on Deviance*, Jack D. Douglas, Ed., New York: Random House, 1972, pp. 139–163.

Warren, Carol A. B., and John M. Johnson, "A Critique of Labeling Theory from the Phenomenological Perspective," in *Theoretical Perspectives on Deviance*, Jack D. Douglas and Robert M. Scott, Eds., New York: Basic Books, 1972, pp. 69–72.

Warren, Carol A. B., "The Use of Stigmatizing Social Labels in Conventionalizing Deviant Behavior," paper read at the Society for the Study of Social Problems annual meeting, New York, August, 1973. To be published in *Sociology and Social Research*, forthcoming.

Weinberg, Martin, S., "The Male Homosexual: Age-Related Variations in Social and Psychological Characteristics," *Social Problems*, **17**:2, Spring, 1970, pp. 527–535.

Westwood, Gordon, *Society and the Homosexual*, New York: E. P. Dutton, 1953.

INDEX